HOW TO VISIT THE BEAUTIES OF

FLORENCE

Pratical guide-book with about 130 illustratitons in black
and white and in colour whith a monumental plan of the city

BONECHI · EDIZIONI "IL TURISMO" · FIRENZE
Via dei Rustici, 5 - Telef. 298.181

Finito di Stampare a Firenze nel 1967

Arti Grafiche PARIGI & MAGGIORELLI
Via F. Caracciolo, 2 - FIRENZE

Impianto Offset
eseguito dalla ditta « LA FOTOLITOGRAFIA »
FIRENZE

Welcome to Florence

Welcome, my friend, to « the heart of the world ».

You will happily find in this carefully prepared guidebook, through the medium of its clear explanations and beautiful pictures, the history, the spirit and the personality of our lovely City of Florence, the priceless gem of Tuscany.

Yes, you can vividly imagine Florence seen from one of the loftly windows of the Palazzo Vecchio or from the topmost cell of Giotto's Campanile during a lovely summer's sunset; you can meditatively admire her on a Spring morning in the luminous apotheosis of San Miniato al Monte; or graciously meet her for the first time or pleasantly recall her from afar by just turning the pages of this booklet.

Florence will invariably char mher visitor with irresistable appleals to again return, and she will always uniquely greet you in the welcome of her ancient streets, in the polychromatism of the churches and monuments, in the phosphorescence of her river. and in the cheerful serenty of her peuple.

Welcome to Florence

Historical note on the city of Florence

Already a flourishing Roman town in the Ist century B.C., Florence later acquired a preeminent position among the cities of Tuscany, especially from the III century A.D., as the seat of the « Corrector Italiae ». The city survived through the time of the Carolingian emperors, becoming one of the most important centres of the peninsula, also from a cultural point of view. First a feudal possession of the Marquesses of Tuscany, among whom may be mentioned Ugo and Matilda, from the XI century onwards Florence acquired an increasing autonomy; in 115, at the end of the struggle against the simoniacal clergy and the feudal lords of the neighbourhood, the Commune of Florence was virtually constituted. Ten years later the new state conquered its rival Fiesole. Soon afterwards inside the city, which was by now surrounded by new walls, the first signs could be seen of a struggle between the city-dwelling feudal lords and the artisan classes, organised into the Arti or tradë corporations. First the struggle took its name from the Ghibellines, the imperial party, and their adversaries the Guelphs. party, the Whites and the Blacks. In 1303 the latter, with the help of the Pope, exiled the Whites from the city. Dante was among those exiled. Meanwhile Florence increased external power fighting against her rival cities (Pistoia, Arezzo, Volterra, Siena) and increasing her territory.

Between the end of the 13th and the early years of the 14th centuries Florence was also becoming one of most important economic and cultural centres of Italy.

This was the age of Dante, of great companies of bankers and merchants, of great wool and silk industries. In the first decades of the 14 century Florence went through various political and economic adventures; first in the struggle against the last Ghibellines, then during the Signoria or rules of Charles of Calabria and Gualtieri di Brienne, duke of Athens (1343). In 1348 there was the terrible plague described by Boccaccio. The last decades of the 14th century saw increasing violent disputes between the high middle class of « fat people », who ruled the state through the greater trade guilds, and the « small people ».

The struggle culminated in the Tumult of the Ciompi (1372), humble workers in the woolmerchants guild, by means of which the lower classes of the city obtained the government. But soon the oligarchy, headed by the Albizi family, got the better of them, Meanwhile supported by the « small people », the rich family of the Medici was acquiring increasing political influence. Soon was founded the Signoria, which, however, preserved a republican appearance. The founder of the Medici rule, Cosimo the Elder, was succeeded by Lorenzo, afterwards called the Magnifico, an astute politician and great patron of the arts. This century, which culminated in the rule of the Magnico (died 1492) into one of the

Meeting of Dante and Beatrice.

brightest in Florentine history, specially in the field of culture and of arts, is the age of Humanism, which had its birthplace in Florence, and of the great art of the Renaissance.

For a few years more, between the end of the 15th century and the beginning of the 16th, the city became a free republic, after the defeat of Piero, the successor of Lorenzo. This glorious period is dominated by the figure of Girolamo Savonarola. When the Medicis returned Florence was under their rule until 1527, when a fresh insurrection gave the longed-for republican form back to the city. But the Medicis, supported by the Emperor and the Pope, returned in 1530 after a very hard siege. Despite its troubled political life, the end of the 15th and the beginning of the 16th centuries are rich in great personalities in the artistic and literary fields (Michelangelo, Machiavelli, Guicciardini). in 1569 Cosimo dei Medici, the ruler of the city, had the title of Grand Duke of Tuscany, which passed to his successors until the extiction of the dynasty with Giangastone in 1737. The Medicis were succeeded by the Lorraine family, which ruled the Grand Duchy, except during the period of the Napoleonic domination. (1799 1814), until the union of Florence and Tuscany to Italy in 1859. Florence was the capital of Italy from 1865 to 1871.

5

INDEX OF ITINERARIES

SUBJECT INDEX

Museum, Galleries, Churches, Palaces, Monuments, etc.

The Baptistery of Saint John the Baptist.

BAPTISTERY. — Lorenzo Ghiberti: « The door of Paradise ».

FIRST ITINERARY

Piazza del Duomo - Baptistry - Cathedral - Cathedral Museum - Palazzo Medici-Riccardi - Church of San Lorenzo - Medici Chapel.

PIAZZA DEL DUOMO. — This square, together with Piazza San Giovanni around the Baptistery, constitutes the centre of the city. The religious monuments found here are: the Baptistery, the Cathedral and the Campanile of Giotto, magnificently harmonized through the polychrome effect of white, green and rose marbles distributed in a rigorously geometric fashion. On Holly Saturdy the characteristic and traditional « scoppio del carro » (a symbolic ceremony) takes place in the square.

THE BAPTISTRY

The Baptistery, which Dante called « il mio bel San Giovanni » and in which he was baptized, is the oldest contruction in Florence. It stands on the ruins of a Paleo Christian monument in the foundations of which were found traces of Roman construction. It is an example of Tuscan Romanesque architecture built on an octagonal plan with coloured marbles. It was dedicated to Saint John the Baptist and was the cathedral of Florence until 1128. The three doors are located at the cardinal points

Andrea Pisano: The Southern Door.   **Lorenzo Ghiberti:** The Northern Door.

of the building. The oldest door, the South, was modelled by Andrea da Pontedera, called il Pisano (1330-36) and cast by the Venetian, Leonardo D'Avanzano. It is divided into 28 sections on which can be found stories from the life' of Saint John the Baptist and *allegories of the cardinal* and *theological virtues.* On either side are Roman sarcophagi with funerary allegories. The North door is the work of Lorenzo Ghiberti (1403-24), with the assistance of Donatello, Paolo Uccello, Bernardo Ciuffagni and Bernardo Cennini. Maintaining the South door's division into 28 sections, he has given to the *stories from the New Testament,* the *Gospels,* and the Doctors of the Church, a new Renaissance character through his naturalistic interpretation. The East door, in front of the Cathedral, was called by Michelangelo « the door of Paradise. » It is the masterpiece of Lorenzo Ghiberti who completed it in 27 years, from 1425 to 1452, imparting to it all of the riches of his imagination, an elegance of composition, and great modelling experience. The stupendous work, an object of constant wonder, has recently been restored to the splendour of its ancient gilding. The door is sub-divided into panels representing biblical scenes from themes ordered by Leonardo Bruni, then Chancellor of the Republic. They are beginning from the top:

11

1 Creation of Adam and Eve; The Original Sin; Expulsion from Paradise.

2 Adam and Eve with Cain and Abel; The Sacrifice to God; The first work: Abel shepherd, Cain at the plough; Cain kills Abel; First example of justice: the Curse of Cain.

3 Story of Noah: His family leaves the ark after the Flood; Noah's thanksgiving and the Rainbow; The planting of the Vine and Noah's drunkenness; derided by Ham he is covered by Shem and Japhet.

4 Story of Abraham; Sara at the entrance to the tent; Angels appear to Abraham in the valley of Mambre; Journey with Isaac to the Mountain; Angel holds Abraham's arm; The servants await their return.

5 Story of Jacob and Esau: Esau sells his first birthright; Isaac sends Esau hunting; Jacob brings the meat to his Father and covers his neck with the skin; Isaac mistakes Jacob for Esau and blesses him; Jacob leaves his Father's house.

6 Story of Joseph: He is put by his brothers in the well; Is sold to the merchants; Is sold by the merchants to Pharaoh; Whose dreams he interprets and foretells the coming famine, counsels provisions; He recognises his brothers and pardons them; Meeting of Joseph and Jacob.

7 Story of Moses: He receives the Tablets of the Law; Joshua waits half way up the mountain; The Israelites wait in fear and trembling at the foot.

8 Story of Joshua: The crossing of the Jordan; The twelve stones taken from the river; The fall of the walls of Jericho; The Israelites take the city.

9 Story of Saul and David: Saul conquers the Philistines; David kills Goliath; And exulting carries the head to the Army.

10 King Solomon solemnly receives the Queen of Sheba.

In the frames of the two doors Ghiberti placed 24 statuettes of Prophets and Sybils alternately with 24 medallions representing artists who were contemporaries of Ghiberti.
LEFT SIDE. Above, the reclining figure represents Spring.
From top to bottom, left: the prophet Amos, the prophet Zacariah, the prophet Daniel, the daughter of Jephtha, Judith.
From top to bottom, right: the prophet Barue, the prophet Elias, the Delphic Sybil, the prophet Isaia, the prophet Haggai.
At the bottom, the reclining figure represents Summer.
RIGHT SIDE. Above, the reclining figure represents Autumn.
From top to bottom left: The Tiberine Sybil, the Persian Sybil, The prophet Elisha, Joshua, the Cuman Sybil.
From top to bottom, right: Judas Maccabeus, Samson, The prophet Jeremiah, Gideon, the prophet Ezechiel.
At the bottom, the reclining figure represents Winter.
The small head almost in the centre of the door, between the Delphic Sybil and the Prophet Isaiah is the self-portrait of Ghiberti. The other between the prophet Elisha and the prophet Joshua, is the portrait of Bartoluccio, step-father of Lorenzo Ghiberti and his master.
Above the door: « The Baptism of Christ » by Andrea Sansovino (1502), the angel is the work of Innocenzo Spinazzi of the 13th century, while the two porphyry columns beside the door, were given to the Florentines by the Pisans in 1117 in gratitude for their generous action while the Pisans were engaged in the war against the Saracens.

13

The Baptistery of Saint John the Baptist. — Interior.

THE INTERIOR of the Baptistry is covered with white and green marbles as is the outside: the cupola is a marvel of Venetian mosaic of the 13th century. Some Florentine artists, and perhaps Cimabue, also worked on them. They show the *Celestial Hierarchies, scenes from the Old Testament,* and the *Last Judgment.* In the centre is the large, solemn *figure of Christ.* On the pavement are the signs of the zodiac and designs inspired by oriental textiles (13th century). The baptismal font is the work of a Pisan sculptor (1371). The fresco on the wall, the Baptism of Christ, is by Alessandro Allori (1531). Left of the entrance we see the *Tomb of Giovanni XXIII,* by Donatello and Michelozzo (1427). Next to the altar the *Angel holding the Candlestick* is by Agostino di Jacopo (1320). To the left between the two Roman sarcophagi, is the *Magdalen* by Donatello (about 1460), famous statue of powerful expression in wood.

THE CATHEDRAL

The work on it was begun by Arnolfo di Cambio in approximately 1296 over the site of the church Santa Reparata, once the cathedral of Florence, opposite the Baptistry. At the death of Arnolfo in 1301, Giotto, who was building the Campanile at the time, assumed the direction of the work. When he died it was continued by Andrea Pisano, then by Francesco Talenti who completed it in 1369, leaving, however, the cupola uncovered. In 1420 a competition was declared for its completion; the competition was won by Filippo Brunelleschi who realized that extraordinary architectural monument admired by the entire world. It took him 14 years, and in 1346 Pope Eugene IV consecrated the cathedral, dedicating it to Santa Maria del Fiore. The present facade was designed in 1887 by the architect De Fabris. The centre door and the two doors on the left are by Passaglia; the right door by Cassioli. Passing along the right side of the cathedral is the so-called DOOR OF THE CANONS, an interesting work by Giovanni d'Ambrogio and Piero di Giovan Tedesco, of the end of the 12th century. Continuing behind the huge architectonic structure of the apse, we reach the left side where we can admire the DOOR OF THE ALMOND, on which we can see Renaissance influences in the *Madonna* by Nanni di Banco and in the two small statues of Prophets by the young Donatello.

THE INTERIOR, divided into three naves by solid and nevertheless elegant pilasters which support the large ogival vaults, is a magnificent example of Florentine-Gothic architecture. It is 150 metres in length, with the nave 33 metres wide and the transept approximately 95. The beautiful stainedglass windows are designed from cartoons by Lorenzo Ghiberti, Agnolo Gaddi, Ambrogio da Pisa, and others. The floor of polychrome marble is attributed to Baccio d'Agnolo and Francesco da Sangallo, and dates from the 16th and 17th centuries. The mosaic on the back wall is attributed to Gaddo Gaddi (14th century); the *Angels Playing* in the six arcades are frescoes by Santi di Tito (16th century), and the *Heads of Prophets* in the clock are by Paolo Uccello (1443). To the right of the central door is the *tomb of Antonio d'Orso* by the Sienese, Tino di Camaiano. In the right nave, the medallion with the *bust of Brunelleschi* is by Andrea Cavalcanti, called il Buggiano (1447); further on is the *bust of Giotto* by Benedetto da Maiano (1490) with an epigraph by Poliziano; in the recess is the *bust of Marsilio Ficino* by Andrea Ferrucci (1521). The cupola excluding the lantern, is 90 metres high, and including the lantern 116; the diameter over the drum is 45 and one half metres. It was covered with frescoes by Gior-

THE CATHEDRAL. — Michelangelo: « Pietà ».

The Baptistery, Duomo and Giotto's Campanile.

gio Vasari and Federico Zuccari toward the end of the 16th century with subjects from the *Last Judgment*. The round glass windows, from cartoons by Paolo Uccello, Lorenzo Ghiberti, Donatello, and Andrea del Castagno, are exceptionally beautiful. Below, the marble choir-stalls, designed by Giuliano di Baccio d'Agnolo, have at their centre the altar, designed by the same, with figures and bas-reliefs by Baccio Bandinelli. (1555). The *Crucifix* is by Benedetto da Maiano (1497). At the end of the transept to the right is an altar dedicated to the Madonna, and, going toward the apse, the door of the *Old Sacristy*, or the *Canons' Sacristy* with a lunette by Luca della Robbia representing the *Ascension* (1454). In the Tribune of San Zanobi there is an urn containing the remains of the Saint: the lovely bas-relief is by Lorenzo Ghiberti (1442). To the left is the *New Sacristy*, or *Chapel of the Mass*, where Lorenzo il Magnifico, fleeing members of the Pazzi Conspiracy which killed his brother Giuliano, took refuge on April 26, 1478. In the lunette the *Resurrection* is by Luca della Robbia (1444). Inside the Sacristy the basin is by Buggiano (1440). In the first chapel of the transept is the dramatic marble *Pietà* by Michelangelo, a work executed by the artist to be put on his tomb and left unfinished in 1555; it is the most important monument in the Cathedral. In the left nave the painting of Dante, the *Divine Comedy* and the *panorama of Florence* is by Domenico di Michelino; the *statue of David* by Bernardo Ciuffagni (1434). There are two important frescoes: an *equestrian portrait of Giovanni Acuto* (John Hawkwood) by Paolo Uccello (1436) and the other of the *soldier Niccolo Marrucci da Tolentino* by Andrea del Castagno (1456).

THE CAMPANILE OF GIOTTO

After more than five hundred years since it was built, this tower is still without an equal of its kind.. Giotto presented the design for it in 1334, on invitation from the Signoria, and in July of the same year the first foundations of the colossal work were laid. Unfortunately Giotto died three years later, and the work was continued until 1348 by Andrea Pisano, then finished by Francesco Talenti in 1359; both scrupulously followed the design of the great master, except for a spire

THE CATHEDRAL. — Interior.

which was never built and which would have added
another thirty metres to the present eighty-four. The
tower is covered in coloured marble and adorned-with
bas-reliefs which may be considered unique in Italy.
The rectangular base is divided into two zones; in
the first are the panels with bas-reliefs by Andrea Pisano and Luca della Robbia after Giotto's design, representing the *History of Human Labour;* in the second
are symbolical figures by Andrea Pisano and Andrea
Orcagna. Then there is the part by Francesco Talenti
with the sixteen niches formerly containing sculptures
by Donatello, Nanni di Bartolo and others, which are

19

THE CATHEDRAL. — **Domenico di Michelino:** « Dante explaining his Divine Comedy ».

now in the Museo dell'Opera del Duomo (Cathedral Museum). The tower then has two zones of two-lighted windows, and a final zone with a threelighted window above which is a projecting cornice with a balustrade; the whole of classic elegance. The Campanile is 81,75m high, and from its top, which can be reached by mounting the stairs with 414 steps, one can enjoy a most wonderful panorama over the whole city and its hills.

LOGGIA DEL BIGALLO. — Facing the Campanile, on the right side of the square, is the characteristic Bigallo palace with its gracious Florentine-Gothic loggia. Attributed to the sculptor and painter Arnoldo Arnoldi, it has three tabernacles on its facade with statues of the Pisan School of the 12th century. On the lunette, a bas-relief by Arnoldi. Inside, of particular interest, is the *Madonna della Misericordia* with a background of 12th century Florence.

THE CATHEDRAL. — **Filippo Brunelleschi:** The Cupola. ▶

CATHEDRAL MUSEUM. — Luca della Robbia: Choir Gallery.

CATHEDRAL MUSEUM (OPERA DEL DUOMO)

In the Museum are Romanesque architectural fragments, statues and decorations which were on the old facade of the Cathedral and in the Baptistry.

Crossing the vestibule, one goes up to the first room containing coats of arms and fragments leading to a large room where are the statues once on the facade of the Cathedral: worthy of note are the *Saint John* by Donatello, the *Saint Luke* by Nanni di Banco, and the *Saint Matthew* by Bernardo Ciuffagni. At the end is the *statue of Boniface VIII* from the work-shop of Arnolfo di Cambio; also by Arnolfo is the *Madonna with Child* on the third wall. Provisionally placed in the centre of the room are the large tables from the choir-galleries, in a room on the floor above. From a door in the fourth wall 'one can reach a small room containing illuminated missals of various centuries, precious reliquaries, enamels and other valuable objects coming from the Cathedral. On the next floor is the Room of the Choir-galleries. To the left, the choir-gallery by Luca della Robbia (1431-38) with *ten reliefs of singing children;* opposite, the choir-gallery by Donatello (1433-38) *with winged, dancing putti* (children). In the same room is the *Moses Jeremiah and Habakkuk* (called lo Zuccone) also by Donatello: they were once in recesses in the Campanile. There is also the Sacrifice of Isaac by Donatello and

22

Médici-Riccardi Palace
by Michelozzo.

Filippo Lippi:
« Madonna and Child ».

Nanni di Bartolo. In the adjoining room is the famous *silver reredos of Saint John the Baptist*, a masterpiece of craftsmanship, completed by the best goldsmiths in Florence after 114 years of work in the 14th and 15th centuries.

On coming out of the Museum, one can turn left, and, following the side of the cathedral, we are soon on a level with the facade.

VIA DE' MARTELLI. — Turning right, one comes into Via de' Martelli; meeting place of the people of Florence and one of the most lively streets of the town. On the right is the Martelli Palace (now a school), and further on, where a recess forms a small square, is the church of S. Giovannino whose facade is by Ammannati (16th cent.). In the interior there are paintings by 16th and 17th century artists. On the corner opposite, where the street changes its name to Via Cavour, is the Medici-Riccardi Palace.

MEDICI-RICCARDI PALACE

This beautiful edifice in pure Renaissance style was commissioned to Michelozzo Michelozzi by Cosimo il Vecchio. The former, a student of Brunelleschi, achieved in this buildings his architectural masterpiece (1444-60). The porticoed courtyard is adorned by graffiti medail-

lions, and has a floor or two-lighted windows and a loggia. In 1659 the palace was acquired by the Riccardi family, who enlarged it in the back. In 1814 it became the property of the State, and is now the residence of the Prefettura.

From the courtyard, on the left, one can reach the MEDICI MUSEUM which contains objets d'art and ornaments belonging to the Medici family. Of particular interest

MEDICI-RICCARDI PALACE. — Benozzo Gozzoli: « Voyage of the Three Kings ». (Detail).

is the *Madonna* by Filippo Lippi (circa 1450), the *funeral mask of Lorenzo,* and numerous small Medici portraits by Bronzino. Back in the courtyard, climbing the right stairway, one can reach the chapel, a true and wondrous jewel of colours, entirely covered with frescoes by Benozzo Gozzoli (1459). The great fresco depicts the *Voyage of the Three Kings;* the youngest king is a portrait of Lorenzo il Magnifico as a young man. On the

Church of San Lorenzo.

altar a *Madonna in Adoration,* a free copy by Neri di Bicci from an original by Filippo Lippi. There is also a gallery in the palace, covered with frescoes by Luca Giordano, with the *Apotheosis of the Medici,* of great compositional effect.

PIAZZA SAN LORENZO. — Enlivened and made very picturesque by the varied market, the piazza is dominated by the huge church of San Lorenzo, behind which rises the cupola of the Princes' Chapel. In front of the church there stands a monument to Giovanni delle Bande Nere. This and the bas-reliefs below it are by Baccio Bandinelli (1540).

CHURCH OF SAN LORENZO

The origins of this church are very ancient in that it began as a church consecrated by Saint Ambrose, Bishop of Milan, in 393. It was rebuilt in Romanesque style around 1000, and again reconstructed along the lines of what we see today, by Filippo Brunelleschi (1421-46), commissioned by Giovanni Bicci de' Medici. The work was completed by his pupil Antonio Manetti in 1460. Also commissioned by the Medici, Michelangelo designed the internal facade, THE NEW SACRISTY AND THE LIBRARY; he had a plan for the external facade, but it was never carried out.

THE INTERIOR is in three naves divided by Corinthian columns; it has an agile and elegant rhythm with its round arcades built upon one curve. The two pulpits, in the last two bays of the central nave, are the last works of Donatello who died in 1466, leaving them unfinished. At the end of the right nave is a marble tabernacle by Desiderio da Settignano. At the foot of the main altar are three bronze grates which designate the burial place of Cosimo il Vecchio dei Medici, called Pater Patriae. The old sacristy, at the corner of the left wing of the transept was created by Brunelleschi. Inside, the *bust of Saint Laurence* is by Donatello, and also by him are the medaillions and lunettes of the Cupola. In the central *sarcophagus*, sculpted by Andrea Cavalcanti called il Buggiano, are buried Giovanni de' Bicci de' Medici, the father of Cosimo il Vecchio and his wife Piccarda. The left *sarcophagus*, under the arch, in porphyry and bronze is the work of Verrocchio and in it are buried Giovanni and Piero de' Medici, sons of Cosimo il Vecchio. Going back to the church, in the Martelli Chapel is the *tomb* of Donatello by Romanelli (1896) and a beautiful *Annunciation* by Filippo Lippi. From the side door of the Chapel one can reach the LARGE CLOISTER, Brunelleschian in style; at the top of the stairs is the LAURENTIAN LIBRARY, founded by Cosimo il Vecchio. Following in its architecture and decoration designs by Michelangelo, it contains an extremely precious and splendid collection of codices and manuscripts and illuminated missals, apart form the *prayerbook* of Lorenzo il Magnifico and a very important collection of autograph manuscripts representing personalities from Petrarch to Napoleon.

CHURCH OF SAN LORENZO. — Interior.

MEDICI CHAPELS. — The Tombs of the Princes.

MEDICI CHAPELS

This remarkable edifice was begun in 1604 by Matteo
Nigetti, following the design of Prince Giovanni de' Medici. The grandiose chapel is octagonal in form with a
cupola over it. The walls are entirely covered with precious marbles, finely worked stones, and gilded bronzes.
On the lower section of the walls are the 16 coats of
arms of the Grand Duchy, in mosaics of marble and
precious stones. The six porphry sarcophagi and statues
belong to the Medici Grand Dukes from Cosimo I to
Cosimo III. The bronze statues are by Pietro Tacca.
Behind the richly decorated altar in semi-precious stones, two small chapels preserve ancient reliquaries and
golden objects of great value. Turning back to the entrance wall to the left, one reaches the NEW SACRISTY,
by Michelangelo (1520) both in its architecture and its
sculptures. Here are the three famous tombs, only two of
which were completed. Near the wall to the left entrance is the *tomb of Lorenzo, Duke of Urbino*, with the
two figures recumbent on the sarcophagus symbolizing
Dawn and Dusk. Opposite is the *tomb of Giuliano,
Duke of Nemours* and, at either end the two symbolic
figures. *Day and Night*. Near the right wall is the mo-

MEDICI CHAPELS. — Pietro Benvenuti: Frescoes in the Cupola.

nument where Lorenzo il Magnifico and his brother Giuliano are buried; to have been dedicated to them, it was not completed. Michelangelo sculpted the *Madonna and Child*.

Medici Chapels.

Michelangelo:
Tomb of Lorenzo, Duke of Urbino.

Michelangelo: Tomb
of Giuliano, Duke of Nemours.

SECOND ITINERARY

Piazza del Duomo - Church of Orsanmichele - Piazza della Signoria - Palazzo della Signoria or Palazzo Vecchio - Uffizi Gallery.

VIA DE' CALZAIUOLI. — On the campanile side of the Duomo, Via de' Calzaiuoli leads away from the piazza. One of the main streets of the town, it joins Piazza del Duomo with Piazza della Signoria, and is the old street of stocking makers and their merchants. It is lined with shops, and soon after entering the street one finds a tablet which indicates where Donatello and Michelozzo had their workshops. Soon after passing Via Tosinghi there is a crossroad. To the left is Via del Corso (the old street where horse races took place), and to the right Via degli Speziali which leads to the modern Piazza della Repubblica. Continuing in the direction of Piazza della Signoria, one comes upon a square, gothic building, somewhat similar to a keep, whose construction resembles more a civic building than a religious edifice. It is the church of Orsanmichele.

CHURCH OF ORSANMICHELE

It is a square Gothic structure almost like a large, low tower. It was actually built as a granary by Arnolfo di Cambio in circa 1290. He demolished the ancient church of Saint Michael Archangel flanked by an orchard (hence called San Michele in Orto). When Arnolfo's church was destroyed by a fire it was reconstructed in the 14th century by the same architects who were building many other buildings in the city: Francesco Talenti, Neri di Fioravante, Benci di Cione and Simone di Francesco Talenti. They put up the one floor loggia to be used as a granary. In 1387 Simone Talenti closed off the arcades. He fulfilled his task amazingly well by closing them with beautiful portals adorned with three-

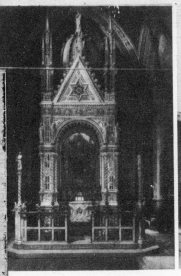

A. Orcagna: The Tabernacle.   Church of Orsanmichele.

light windows as light as lace, while placing in the tabernacles behind the pilasters, statues of the patron saints of the guilds of the Arti Maggiori.

Beginning from Via Calzaiuoli, we find: *Saint John the Baptist* by Ghiberti (1414-16); *Christ and Saint Thomas* by Andrea del Verrocchio (1464-83); *Saint Luke* by Giambologna (1601); *Saint Philip* by Nanni di Banco (1405-10); *four crowned Saints* by Nanni di Banco (1408); *Saint George* by Donatello (copy); *Saint Matthew* by Lorenzo Ghiberti (1420); *Saint Stephen* by Lorenzo Ghiberti (1426-28); *Saint Eligio* by Nanni di Banco (1415); *Saint Mark* by Donatello (1411-13); *Saint Jacob* attributed to Ciuffagni; *Madonna of the Rose* attributed to Simone Talenti; *Saint John the Evangelist* by Baccio da Montelupo (1516). Inside, the pilasters and vaults are decorated with frescoes of the 13th and 14th centuries dedicated to the patron saints of the guild of the Arti Minori, and there are polychrome windows. But the extraordinary *Tabernacle* by Andrea di Cione called Orcagna (1335-59) dominates the interior with its elegant richness of statuettes, arabesques, angels, saints, and beautiful bas-reliefs of Scenes from the *Life of Mary*. A true masterpiece it is, of high Gothic. Among the bas-reliefs the most interesting is the

PIAZZA DELLA SIGNORIA. — **Bartolomeo Ammannati:** Neptune

death of Mary and her *Assumption*, behind the altar. The tabernacle serves as a baldachin to a Giotto-like painting called *Madonna of the Graces*, attributed to Bernardo Daddi.

PIAZZA DELLA SIGNORIA

This square is of incomparable beauty and solemnity with the Palazzo della Signoria, the Loggia dei Lanzi, the ancient buildings, the large fountain and the monuments standing there which all create an unforgettable impression of greatness and power. Here, in fact, for centuries and centuries took place the great historical and political events, and here was delineated all Florentine life, in its internal rivalries, its affirmations of prestige and its messages of civilization brought to the world.

PIAZZA DELLA SIGNORIA. — **Palazzo della Signoria (or Palazzo Vecchio).**

On the left side of the square, the *equestian statue of Cosimo I dei Medici* is by Giambologna. Beside the Palazzo della Signoria is the fountain with the gigantic *Neptune* by Bartolomeo Ammannati (1563-75), a work generally not held in very high esteem. In front of the Palace, on a level with the stairway, are arranged several important sculptures. On the left: *the Marzocco* by Donatello, a stone copy of the original in the National Museum; *Judith and Holofernes* by Donatello (1460); the copy of Michelangelo's *David*, in the Galleria dell'Accademia; and finally *Hercules and Cacus*, by Baccio Bandinelli.

LOGGIA DELLA SIGNORIA

To the right of the Palace is the elegant and airy Loggia della Signoria, a rare example of late Gothic with foreshadowings of the Renaissance. It was also called LOGGIA DEI LANZI because it was the headquarter of the Landesknechts during the time of the Grand Duchy, and LOGGIA DELL'ORCAGNA from a design supposedly by that artist; actually it was built by the same architects who supervised the construction of the Cathedral, Benci di Cione, Simone Talenti and others, from the years 1376-82. At the sides of the entrance delimiting it are *two marble lions,* one by Vacca (1600) and one older. Under the loggia are arranged ancient *Roman sculptures* and 16th century works of Florentine sculptors. Among them, in the left arch, *Perseus,* the bronze masterpiece of Benvenuto Cellini (1553); *the Rape of the Sabine women* by Giambologna (1583); and *Hercules and the Centaur also* by Giambologna (1599). The group, *Menelaus and Patroclus,* is a restored copy from a Greek original of the 4th century B.C., and the *Rape of Polixena,* is a 19th century work of the sculptor Pio Fedi (1866).

PALAZZO DELLA SIGNORIA

It stands before us majestic and severe in its imposing majesty. It was also called PALAZZO VECCHIO after Cosimo moved here with his family in 1550. The tower is 94 metres high and ,jutting up directly from the facade in an exceptionally daring architectural manoeuvre, it gives a particular elegance to the severe building. Arnolfo di Cambio (1232-1301) is said to have been its architect, using as his model the castle of the Counts Guidi di Poppi. It is certain that the building of the castle dates back to the period between the end of the 13th and beginning of the 14th centuries, but it took additional centuries to complete it. The building, studded with bosses, with its beautiful two-fold windows on the two floors, ends in a gallery with battlements, from the side of which rises the tower; it was constructed laterally over a pre-existing Tower of the Foraboschi. On the door there is a frieze with two lions and at the centre the sign of Christ by Saint Bernardino.

INTERIOR. - Entering by the main door, our attention is dominated by the harmonious and suggestive beauty of the courtyard by Michelozzo Michelozzi (1435), with at its centre the exceptional graceful small *winged Cupid with Fish,* by Andrea Verrocchio (1476), the original of which is in the Chapellor's Room. From the courtyard, going up the two stairways we reach the SALONE DEI CINQUECENTO (Room of the Five Hundred),built by Simone del Pollaiolo, called il Cronaca, and definitively arranged by Giorgio Vasari who covered the vast walls with *frescoes of the battles* fought by Cosimo I. The ceiling, divided into 39 richly framed sections, has the same number of panels, painted by Vasari and assistants; at the centre is the *Triumph of Cosimo I.* Along the walls are six marble groups with the *Labors of Hercules,* by Vincenzo de' Rossi. At the front wall is the marble group, *Genius conquering Brute Force,* by Michelangelo. Through the little door to the right of the entrance wall one can enter the STUDY OF FRANCESCO I: a small, gracious room adorned by paintings, frescoes and small bronze statues and decored with stuccoes and carvings, designed by Vasari for the prince's relaxation. Returning to the Salone del Cinquecento, we enter the VESTIBULE decorated by Lorenzo Sabatini leading into the SALA DEI DUECENTO (Room of the Two Hundred). It was built from 1475 to 1480 by Benedetto and Giuliano da Maiano. There are magnificent Florentine tapestries on the walls. Turning back, we reach, through a door in the back on the left, a series of rooms, each one dedicated to a member of the Medici family and decorated with frescoes by Vasari and his assistants. Going up to the second floor, we reach the ensemble of rooms named

Loggia della Signoria.

Pio Fedi:
« The Rape of Polyxena »

Menelaus and Patroclus.

Giambologna:
« Rape of the Sabine Women ».

Giambologna:
« Hercules and the Centaur ».

Benvenuto Cellini: « The Perseus »

after the Elements, built by Bernardo del Tasso and thus called from its frescoes by Vasari and Cristoforo Gherardi, called il Doceno. We then pass to the TERRACE OF SATURN from which we enjoy a beautiful view of Florence and its hills. Following it are the ROOM OF HERCULES, the TERRACE OF JUNO (now called the Terrace of Jove), the ROOM OF CYBELE, the ROOM OF CERES and the ROOM OF CALLIOPE. We pass from here into the apartments of Eleanor of Toledo, the consort of Cosimo I, especially prepared for her by Vasari (1562). A small vestibule leads to the GREEN ROOM on the left of which is a CHAPEL painted by Bronzino; from here we pass into Eleanor's four rooms decorated by Vasari and Stradano: the ROOM OF THE SABINES, the ROOM OF ESTHER, the ROOM OF PENELOPE and the ROOM OF GUALDRADA, the private bed-room of the Duchess. In the passage leading to the CHAPEL OF THE SIGNORIA is a mask of Dante. In the Chapel, Girolamo Savonarola passed in prayer the last night before his execution. The frescoes are by Ridolfo del Ghirlandaio (1514) and on the altar there is a *Holy Family* by Mariano da Pescia. Continuing, we pass to the AUDIENCE HALL, the work of Benedetto da Maiano with its magnificent ceiling carved by Giuliano da Maiano. Next is the ROOM OF THE LILIES, with a beautiful doorway by Benedetto da Maiano; above it is a statue of *John the Baptist*. The large fresco on the wall is by Domenico Ghirlandaio (1485). The Medici Wardrobe, also called MAP ROOM, is the one we next encounter. It was thus named because on the doors of the wardrobes are painted 53 maps by Ignazio Danti (1563-75) and don Stefano Buonsignori (1575-84). Returning to the Room of the Lilies one can reach the gallery and from there the top of the tower.

UFFIZI PALACE. — The small Uffizi square is flanked by Vasari's beautiful building and the magnificent final archway looking over the Arno. Grand Duke Cosimo I commissioned Vasari for the building of the imposing edifice, intended as a meeting place for government officials (1570-84). Along the arcade, in the recesses of the internal pillars, were placed, in the middle of the 19th century, statues of Tuscans of that period; one of the sculptors was Giovanni Dupré, sculptor of the *statue of Giotto*.

UFFIZI GALLERY

The gallery is famous throughout the world for its magnificent and vast collection, not only of Florentine and Tuscan paintings of the 14th, 15th and 16th centuries, but also for its distinguished works from the schools of Umbria, Emilia, the Veneto, and other Italian schools which are well represented here. There are also works from other European schools such as the Flemish, French and German, so that, all in all, this gallery can be considered the most important in Italy and one of the most important in the world. The gallery's patrimony comes from the Medici and Lorena collections. Francesco I, a passionate cultivator of the fine arts, employed Bernardo Buontalenti (1574) to arrange the collection; whence the sculptures, once belonging to Cosimo il Vecchio and Lorenzo il Magnifico, were arranged in their proper rooms, together with the extremely rich collection of his father Cosimo I. At the death of Gian Gastone, the last of the Medici, Anna Maria Luisa, the wife of the Palatine Elector and last Medici heir, donated the entire gallery to the Tuscan states with the family pact of 1737, stipulating that the rich collection always remain in Florence.

The entrance to the Gallery is at the beginning of the portico to the left. On both sides of the entrance we see the statues of *Cosimo the Elder* and *Lorenzo il Magnifico*, and in the interior several busts of the Medici family.

From the *Vestibule*, following immediately the entrance, we go up the Gallery over *Vasari's staircase* where various sculptures, ancient copies of Roman and Greek works, can be noted (the lift may be used). Those who walk up (or down the stairs) can visit the CABINET OF DRAWINGS AND PRINTS on the first floor.

On the second floor, through a vestibule adorned with antique statues and sculptures, we reach the FIRST GALLERY. Here we find numerous Roman sarcophagi of the 2nd, 3rd and 4th centuries, B.C., while on the walls we see tapestries representing *Hunting Scenes* of the 15th and 16th centuries. The decorations in the ceiling are mythologic subjects by Allori and other artists of the same period.

We begin our visit returning to the end of the corridor towards the Palazzo Vecchio. Here we reach the HERMAPHRODITE ROOM deriving its name from the reclining Hermaphorodite of the Roman epoch, a copy of a Hellenistic sculpture. Besides this statue note, among the other works, three copies of the Roman epoch of the *Doryforos* (halberbier) by Policlete. Other Roman sculptures of the 1st century B.C. are the *Sacrifice of the Bull* and the *Resting Wayfarer*. Another Roman copy of a Hellenic original is *Hercules defeating the Centaur* restored by Giovanni Caccini at the end of the 16th century; it is in the corridor immediately after leaving the Hermaphrodite Room.

The Uffizi Palace.

ROOM II — Dedicated to Italian painters of the 13th century. We find that the masterpieces of this century take us back to the first master of Italian painting, which, after the breakaway from Bizantine art, became more figurative and humanistic. The great *Crucifix* from Santa Croce dominates this first room. It was painted by Cimabue, a Florentine painter, and is flanked by the *Madonna enthroned and Child* with Angels, by Giotto, the real initiator of Italian painting, who probably painted it between 1303-1305, during the period in which the artist was carrying out the frescoes in Assisi. On the lateral walls two other *Madonnas* complete the masterpieces, one, the *Madonna enthroned with angels and Saints* is also by Cimabue, the other by Duccio di Buoninsegna of the Sienese School. This painting is also called the *Rucellai Madonna* because it came originally from the Rucellai Chapel in Santa Maria Novella. The room is completed by works of the Lucca School, among which are worthy of note, the *Stigmata of St. Francis*, by Bonaventura Berlinghieri, and a diptych of the *Madonna and Child with Saints* of the school of Berlingheri. Notable also are the *St. Luke*, by the Master of the Magdalen, and the *Reedemer between the Virgin, St. Peter, and St. Paul*, by Meliore Toscano. Of the Pisan School are the *Crucifix* and the *Stories of the Passion*, of the 12th century.

ROOM III — 14th century Italian Artists. Here we find Ambrogio and Pietro Lorenzetti, artists of the Sienese School. Of the former there are the *Stories of St. Nicholas of Bari*, the *Presentation in the Temple*, *St. Procolo* and *St. Nicholas;* of Pietro Lorenzetti are the *Stories of the Life of St. Humility*, and a *Madonna with Angels*. Here also are the famous *Annunciation* of Simone Martini, once in the Cathedral of Siena, a work of such subtle grace and poetry as to be considered a real masterpiece, and *St. Ansano and St. Judith* by Lippo Memmi, also of the Sienese School. Besides these there are a *Madonna and Child* by Ser Tozzo Tegliacci, a Nativity by Simon of the Crucifixions, and the *Presentation in the Temple* by Nicholas Buonaccorsi.

UFFIZI GALLERY. — Giotto: « Madonna Enthroned ». ▶

Room IV — In this room also we find 14th century artists mostly of the Florentine School, followers of Giotto. Of Bernardo Daddi, *Madonna and Child, Madonna and Child with Saints, Madonna and Child with Angels*, and the *Stories of the Virgin*. Of Nardo di Cione, called Orcagna, *Crucifixion*. Of Taddeo Gaddi, *Madonna and Child with Angels*. Of Giottino, the *Descent from the Cross*, which clearly shows the remarkable personality of the artist. Of John of Milan, a series of *Saints, Prophets, Patriarchs, Apostles. Martyrs and Virgins*, as well as the *Saint Matthew* of Andrea and Jacopo Orcagna.

Room V and VI — Here we find the artists of the end of the 14th and the beginning of the 15th centuries. Of Gentile da Fabriano is the beautiful *Adoration of the Magi*, in beautiful colours and elegant gothic style, as his other compositions *St. Mary, St. Magdalen, St. Nicholas of Bari, St. John* and *St. George*. By Lorenzo Monaco, influenced by a graceful form of gothic, are the *Crowning of the Virgin* and the *Adoration of the Magi*. By Agnolo Gaddi are a *Crucifixion, Madonna and Child with SS. Peter and Paul Thomas Aquinas, and St. Dominic*. Here also is the *Thebaid* by Gherardo Starnina.

Room VII — Here are brought together the masterpieces of Florentine Painting of the 15th century. The *Madonna and Child of* Fra Angelico, the *Madonna and Child with Saint Anne* by Masaccio and his master Masolino; the well-known *portraits of Frederic of Montefeltro and Battista Sforza with wife;* the celebrated *Battle of San Romano* by Paolo Uccello, recently restored. By Filippino Lippi there are *Saint Frediano deviates the Course of the Serchio, An Angel announces her Death to the Virgin*, and *Saint Augustine in his Study*, also the *Madonna enthroned with Saints* by Domenico Veneziano, which reveals the exceptional gift for colour of the artist.

Room VIII — Dedicated in particular to the artists of the 15th century, Filippo Lippi and his followers. Of the master we have a *Madonna and Child with Saints*, the *Coronation of the Virgin*, a work rich in contemporary portraits, *Virgin Adoring the Child with St. Hilarion, Virgin Adoring the Child with St. Bernard, Madonna and Child with Saints, Annunciation, St. Antony Abbot*, and *St. John the Baptist*. Of the Sienese Lorenzo Vecchietta is the *Virgin and Child with divers Saints*, of Pesellino a scholar of Lippi, the *Miracle of St. Antony*, the *Martyrdom of SS. Cosmo and Damian and the Nativity of Jesus*. Here also we find the beautiful *Coronation of the Virgin* by Fra Angelico. Baldovinetti is represented by an *Annunciation* and a *Virgin and Child with Saints*, and Benozzo Gozzoli with a *Pietà, St. John and St. Mary Magdalen*. The *Stories of St. Benedict* are of the Sienese painter Neroccio di Bartolomeo. By Peter and Antony del Pollaiolo are *St. Vincent, St. James*, and *St. Eustace*, while a *Madonna with Saints* is by Matteo di Giovanni (temporary arrangement).

Room IX — Here are the works of Sandro Filipepi, better known as Botticelli and of the brothers Peters and Antony del Pollaiolo. Of Botticelli are *Fortitude*, the *Portrait of a Young man*, and three beautiful paintings of the *Virgin and Child*. Of the Pollaiolo brothers are the *Six Virtues* and the *portrait of the Duke Galeazzo Sforza* and his wife.

Room X — This is dedicated to Botticelli, represented here with his most important works: the *Madonna of the Pomegranate*, the *Madonna of the Magnificat; Allegory of Spring* (1478), the *Birth of Venus* (1486); these latter two works were painted for the Medici Villa of Castello. The *Annunciation*, the *Madonna and Child with Saints, the Adoration of the Holy Kings* (1474), where the central group, culminating in the Madonna, represents personages of the Medicean Court: Cosimo the Elder, Pietro the Gouty, Lorenzo the Magnificent and others, whilst the figure to the right, (turned towards the public), is the self-portrait of the painter.

Room XI — This little room likewise is mainly dedicated to Botticelli and contains some of his small pictures, among which of particular interest are the *Allegory of Calumny* and *Saint Augustine in his Cell: Saint Augustine and a Child on the Sea Shore;* two paintings by Filippino Lippi, son and scholar of Filippo.

Room XII — This room is dedicated to Mantegna. We admire by this master of the Padoan School the *Adoration of the Kings,* to both sides the *Ascension* and the *Circumcision,* a most beautiful Triptych which reveals completely the master's art. Other works by Mantegna: the *Madonna with Child* and the *Portrait of Cardinal Carlo de Medici. Saint Dominicus* is the work of Cosmé Tura and *Saint Lodovico di Tolosa* is Bartolommeo Vivarini's work, both influenced by Mantegna. The *Pietà* is the work of Lorenzo d'Alessandro.

Room XIII — Dedicated to Flemish painting. It contains the *Laying of Christ in Sepulchre* by *Roger van der Weyden* and some strong *portraits* by Hans Memling, and of the same artist, a *Madonna enthroned with Angels. R.T. Furthermore there are to be seen three* paintings by Filippino Lippi: *Portrait of an old Man,* a *Self Portrait,* fresco on flat-tile and an *Allegory with View of Florence.*

Room XIV — This is dedicated to Hugo Van der Goes. The strong influence of this great Flemish artist on the Florentine painters of the second half of the 15th century is well-known. In this room we see the *Portinari Triptych,* painted in Bruges about 1476 for Tommaso Portinari who donated it to the Church of Sant-Egidio. In this room are other works: the *Tripitych* by the Avignon painter Nicola Fromet; several *Madonnas* by Domenico Ghirlandaio; by Lorenzi di Credi, *Adoration of the Shepherds;* A *Madonna* and an *Adoration of the Holy Kings* by Filippino Lippi. *The three Archangels and Tobias* is Botticini's work.

Room XV — This room is dedicated to Luca Signorelli and Pietro Perugino, Umbrian painters, and it contains some works by Verrocchia, his scholar Lorenzo di Credi, and Piero di Cosimo, Florentine painters. By Signorelli we see the *Holy Family* and *Madonna with Child;* by Verrocchio, master of Leonardo, (but more famous as a sculptor than as a painter), we see the *Baptism of Christ* (1470) executed with the help of the young scholar. The *Annunciation with Stories of the Genesis* is Lorenzo di Credi's work; the *Immaculate Conception* and the *Liberation of Andromeda* are both the works of Pietro di Cosimo, pupil of Cosimo Rosselli who excels by far his master. By Leonardo da Vinci is the *Adoration of the Magi,* executed in 1481 for the monks of the convent of San Donato in Scopeto, but it is un unfinished work. By Lorenzo di Credi; a *Madonna with Child and Saint Mary Magdalen; Madonna and Archangels* by Signorelli. Furthermore the *Madonna with St. John the Baptist and Saint Sebastian* by Perugino.

Room XVI — Or room of the Maps. The maps on the walls are frescoes of the year 1589 by Bonsignori. In this room the *Annunciation* of Leonardo (about 1475).

Room XVII — Dedicated to the Umbrians. It contains paintings of small size by Luca Signorelli: *Scenes of the Birth of Christ, scenes of the Passion* and *Allegory of Fertility.* By Piero di Cosimo: *Madonna and playing Angels; Portrait of a young Man* by

UFFIZI GALLERY. — Simone Martini: « Annunciation ».

Lorenzo di Credi; *Madonna with Child and Angels* by Bartolomeo Caporali. Among the other works belonging to Antoniazzo Romano, Bartolommeo Caporali and Giovanni Boccati, is the most remarkable painting by Melozzo da Forlì representing the half figures of the *Baptist* and of *Saint Benedict* and on the back the *Annunciation*.

Tʀɪʙuɴᴇ — Built by Buontalenti (1589). In the middle of the hall: the *Venus of the Medici*, Hellenic art of the 3rd century B.C. The other sculptures represent: *Torso of a Satry*, sculpture of the Pergamon epoch of the 2nd century B.C.; the *Knife Grinder*, the *Wrestlers, Apollinus, the Faun*, all Roman copies of Hellenic originals. On the walls, starting from the left: *Portrait of Bianca Cappello* by Alessandro Allori; *Portrait of Lorenzo the Magnifico* by Giorgio Vasari; *Portrait of Cosimo the Elder*, by Pontormo; *Portrait of a young Man with book* by Agnolo Bronzino, and by the same artist are: *Portrait of Bartolommeo and Lucrezia Panciatichi, Portrait of Don Francesco dei Medici, Portrait of a Lady, Portrait of Don Garzia dei Medici, Portrait of the Princess Isabelle, Portrait of Eleonora di Toledo and Cosimo I in armour.* The *Portrait of a Gentleman* is by Cecchino Salviati.

44

UFFIZI GALLERY. — **Masaccio and Masolino:** « **Madonna with** Child and St. Anne ». ▶

ROOM XIX — Devoted to Perugino and Francia. Of the first are many portraits among which is the portrait of *Francesco delle Opere*, where the artist expresses himself with absorbed and harmonious sensitivity. Lorenzo Costa and Francesco Francia were influenced by Perugino. Here we see *Saint Sebastian* by Costa and by the same artist: the *Portrait of Giovanni II Bentivoglio*, by Francia the Portrait of *Evangelista Scappi*. Other paintings to be seen here belong to the Bolognese Amico Aspertini and to the Emilian painters Giovan Francesco dei Maineri, Lorenzo Leombruno and Alessandro Araldi.

ROOM XX — Dedicated to Giambellino and to Duerer. Of the Venetian master Giovanni Bellini we see only the *Agony of Christ* (1490) painted in chiaroscuro expressing the sensitive shades of Bellini's art. Among the many works of Durer, influenced by the charm of the Venetian painting, we see *Saint Philip the Apostle* and *Saint James the Apostle*, a *Madonna and Child* (1526), the *Father's Portrait* (1490), the *Adoration of the Magi* (1504), *Calvary* (1505), the *Self-Portrait* and *Adam and Eve*. We have here works by Lucas Cranach, compatriot of Durer and influenced by him; the *Portrait of Luther and his wife*, Portraits of *Luther and Melanchton*, *Saint George* and on the back the *Head of the Saviour*, the *Self-Portrait*, *Adam and Eve*, whilst the *Portrait of Giovanni I* and the *Portrait of Frederic III of Saxony* are works of Cranach's workshop. In this room we find two more paintings, one by the Flemish artist, Gerard David: the *Descent from the Cross;* the other one by the follower of Bellini, Giovanni Monsueti *Christ in the Temple*.

ROOM XXI — Dedicated to Giovanni Bellini, to Giorgione and to the artists influenced by these two great Venetian masters. The *Portrait of a Gentleman* and the *Allegory of the Purgatory* are the works of Giambellino. The fragment of a *Crucifixion* is the work of Vittore Carpaccio representing a group of armed soldiers. Further, Giorgione, the *Judgement of Salomon* and *the Boy Moses before Pharoah* of the beginning of the XVI century and the *Warrior with his groom*. Further, the *Gypsy Girl* by Boccaccio Boccaccino; the *Madonna and Child* and *Saint Peter and the Donor* by Pietro Duja and another; *Madonna and Child* by Cima da Conegliano.

ROOM XXII — This room is devoted to the northern painters of the beginning of the 16th century. We see besides Hans Holbein's best works, the two paintings representing the *Stories of Saint Florian* by Albrecht Altdorfer. *The Adoration of the Magi* is by the Flemish artist Gerard David and it is one of his best works. The eight altar-panels representing *Stories of the Saints Peter and Paul* are the work of Hans Kulmbach, who was much influenced by Durer. The *Madonna with Saint Barbara and Saint Catherine* is attributed to the Antwerp painter, called Master of Hoogstraeten.

ROOM XXIII — Dedicated to Antonio Allegri, called the Correggio. Attracted by Leonardo's charm, Correggio has his own fresh and personal style. Here we find: the *Adoration of the Child, Rest on the Flight to Egypt* (about 1520) and the *Madonna in Glory*, one of his early paintings. *Narcissus at the Fountain* is a work by Boltraffio and the *Portrait of an Unknown and a Lady* are of the flemish painter of the Italian school, Joos Van Cleve. In this room we find various works of Italian and foreign painters influenced by Leonardo. The *Portrait of a Man* is by Bernardino dei Conti; the *Portrait of an Unknown* is by Van Cleve; *Saint Catherine* by Giampietrino; the *Capture of Christ* by Sodoma.

UFFIZI GALLERY. — Gentile da Fabriano: « Adoration of the Magi ».

MINIATURE ROOM — This pretty little room contains numerous miniatures of Italian and Foreign artists between the 15th and the 17th centuries. Originally this hall was the Precious Stone Room (its former contents have now been transferred to the Silver Museum of Palazzo Pitti).

SECOND CORRIDOR — In this corridor, joining the two sides of the building of the Uffizi, note the various sculptures of the Roman epoch: the *Circular Altar with the Sacrifice of Iphigenia*, the *Boy taking a Thorn out of his Foot*, *Venus Bathing*. From the big windows of this corridor we enjoy a marvellous view of the Florentine hills and an impressive picture of the portico of the Uffizi with the Palazzo Vecchio.

THIRD CORRIDOR — In this gallery the famous corridor, built by Vasari in 1564 at order of Cosimo I, opens up, joining Palazzo Pitti with the Uffizi across the Ponte Vecchio. This gallery is open as far as the Ponte Vecchio and contains a part of the large collection of Self-Portraits of Italian and foreign artists. Among them we find self-portraits of Titian, Michelangelo, Raphael, Rubens, Rembrandt, Canova, Fattori, Ensor etc..

The tapestries on the walls of the gallery are subdivided into three series: the first one representing *Scenes from the Passion* are of Florentine manifactures executed from cartoons by Allori and Cigoli; the other two, representing *Stories of Jacob* and *Battles* were manufactured in Brussels in the XVI century. At the beginning of the gallery there are two important statues of the Roman epoch, while at the end we note the *Laocoon* Group of the XVI century by Baccio Bandinelli (copy of the famous Group in the Vatican).

ROOM XXV — This room is dedicated to Raphael and Michelangelo, the great Italian artists of the 16th century. The works by Raphael are: the famous *Madonna of the Goldfinch* (about 1506), the *Portrait of Pope Leo X with the Cardinals Giulio de Medici and Luigi de Rossi* (1518), while the *Portrait of Elisabetta Ganzaga*, the *Portrait of Guidobaldo della Rovere* are attributed to him and the *Portrait of the Pope Jules II* is considered to be a copy

UFFIZI GALLERY. — Botticelli: « Birth of Venus ».

and not the original of the artist. By Michelangelo Buonarroti is the famous round *Holy Family* (1505). *The painting representing Joseph the Patriarch presenting his Father and Brothers to the Pharoah* is by Francesco Granacci; the *Annunciation*, the *Nativity* and the *Presentation in the Temple* are the works of Albertinelli; The *Pietà* and the *Holy Family* by Bronzino; the *Visitation* also by Albertinelli.

ROOM XXVI — Dedicated to Andrea del Sarto. His works are the big altarpiece, the *Madonna of the Harpies*, so called because of the mythological figures around the pedestal, *Saint James and the two Children, Two Angels, Portrait of a young Woman, The four Saints* (Saint Michael Archangel, Saint Giovanni Gualberto, Saint

UFFIZI GALLERY. — Botticelli: « Allegory of Spring ».

UFFIZI GALLERY. — Botticelli: « Judith ». ▶

UFFIZI GALLERY. — **Lorenzo Monaco:** « Adoration of the Magi »

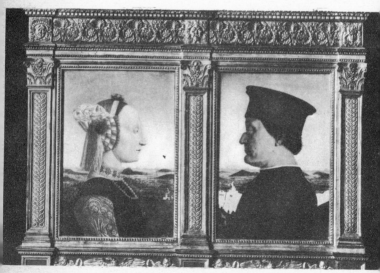

UFFIZI GALLERY. — **Piero della Francesca:** « Federico da Montefeltro and his wife Battista Sforza ».

Bernard of the Uberti and Saint John the Baptist). *Moses defending the daughters of Jethro* and the *Portrait of a young girl* are the works of Rosso Fiorentino; *The Charity* is by Salviati: *Ecce Homo* by Lucas van Lijden; the painting of the *Copper Mines* by Herry van der Cles (called Civetta); the *Portrait of a Woman* and *Adam and Eve driven out of the Garden Eden* are Pontormo's work.

ROOM XXVII — Devoted to Jacopo Carrucci, called il Pontormo. This artist, influenced by Durer and Michelangelo, is here represented by his *Madonna with Child between St. Jerone and Saint Francis*, a *Portrait of a Man*, the *Portrait of Francesco dell'Aiolle*, the *Charity*, the *Supper at Emmaus, Leda and the Swan, Nativity of Saint John the Baptist* The other works are of numerous artists Domenico Beccafumi's *Holy Family;* Bacchiacca's *Stories of Saint Acacio, Christ at Caiphas, Descent from the Cross* and *Archangel Raphael;* Rosso Fiorentino's *Playing Child* and *Enthroned Madonna;* Franciabigio's *Portrait of a young Man*.

ROOM XXVIII — Dedicated to Titian — We see here the following works of the great Venetian painter: *Venus and Cupid*, the *Portrait of Eleonora Gonzaga della Rovere*, the *Knight of Malta*, the famous *Flora* and the *Venus of Urbin*. There is the *Madonna with Child and Saints* by Palma the Elder, follower of Titian, and by the same artist the *Resurrection of Lazzarus* and the *Judith*.

ROOM XXIX — Dedicated to Francesco Mazzola, called the Parmigianino. His masterpieces: the *Madonna with the long Neck* and the *Portrait of a Man*, which at one time was considered to be his self-portrait. Paintings of Ferraresi and Emilian artists are exhibited in this hall, among them by Dosso Dossi, the *Portrait of a Warrior;* by Benvenuto Tisi, called the Garofalo: the *Annunciation*; by Scarsellino (Ippolito Scarsella): the *Judgement of Paris;* by Girolamo Genga: the *Martyrdom of Saint Sebastian;* by Gerolamo da Carpi the *Adoration of the Child* and *Martha and Mary kneeling before the Saviour;* by Lavinia Fontana: *Noli me Tangere;* and by Mazzolino: the *Adoration of the Child* and the *Massacre of the Innocents*.

ROOM XXX — Emilian Hall. Here are exhibited, many works of artists of the preceeding halls among which the *Madonna and Saint Anne* and the *Circumcision* are by Mazzolino; the *Rest in Egypt* by Dosso Dossi; the *Madonna of Saint Zacharias* by Parmigianino; the *Tribute* by Garofalo. The *Vision of Saint Aldegonda* is the work of Battista Dossi, brother of Dosso.

ROOM XXXI — Dedicated to Dosso Dossi (Giovanni Luteri). Of this artist we see *Witchcraft* and the *Madonna in Glory between St. John the Baptist and John the Evangelist*. Interesting is the *Fornarina* by Sebastiano del Piombo, while the *Portrait of a Man is* attributed to him. The *Head of an old Man* is of the Venetian School of the 16th century.

ROOM XXXII — This is devoted to Sebastiano del Piombo. Represented here is his most important work: the *Death of Adonis*. Of special interest among the numerous works of Venetian painters of the 16th century exhibited here are the *Sacred Conversation* by Lorenzo Lotto, two *portraits* by Paris Bordone, two *portraits* by Romanino.

ROOM XXXIII — Corridor of the 16th century. This corridor was built with the intention of reaching directly the following halls. Here are the works of Italian and foreign artists of the 16th cen-

UFFIZI GALLERY. — Raphael: « Madonna of the Bullfinch ».

UFFIZI GALLERY. — Michelangelo: « Holy Family ».

UFFIZI GALLERY. — Tintoretto: « Leda ».

tury, among whom are Vasari, Alessandro Allori, Jacopo Ligozzi, Bronzino, Francois Clouet, Lis Morales etc..

ROOM XXXIV — Dedicated to Paolo Calieri, called the Veronese. Of this great Venetian artist we see: the *Holy Family with Saint Barbara*, *Saint Agatha crowned by Angels*, the *Annunciation*, while the attribution is doubtful regarding the *Martyrdom of Saint Justina* and *Esther and Ahasuerus*. Among the other works we note: the *Transfiguration* by Giovanni Girolamo Savoldi; by the North Italian Giovanni Battista Moroni are: the *Portrait of Giovanni Antonio Pantera*, the *Portrait of Count Piero Secco Suardi* and the *Man with the Book*. Other portraits by the Cremonese Giulio Campi and *Portrait of Man* by Tintoretto.

ROOM XXXV — This is devoted to Tintoretto (Jacopo Robusti) and to Baroccio (Federico Barocci). Tintoretto's works contained in this hall are: the *Portrait of a Man with Red Hair*, the *Leda*, the *Portrait of Jacopo Sansovino*, *Jesus and the Samaritan*, *Portrait of an Admiral*, *Portrait of an old Man in Fur*, *Portrait of a Man*. This latter one is of uncertain attribution. The following works are by Baroccio: *Portrait of a Woman;* the *Stigmata of Saint Francis*, the *Noli me tangere*, the *Portrait of Francesco Maria II della Rovere* and the grandiose *Madonna of the People*. Of considerable importance are the works by Jacopo Bassano and Palma the Younger. The *Burning Wilderness* is by Domenico Tintoretto, son of Jacopo.

ROOM XXXVI — Dedicated to Caravaggio (Michelangelo Merisi), who, about the end of the 16th century, gave impulse to Italian modern art. His are the three canvases representing: the *Young Bacchus*, an early work of this artist, the *Head of Medusa*, painted on a tournament shield and the *Sacrifice of Isaac*. There are also the following interesting works: the *Supper* by von Honthorst, called Gherardo delle Notti; *Salomè* by Battistello; *the Healing of the Obsessed* by Mattia Preti, *Esther and Ahasuerus* by Bernardo Cavallino; the *Summer Resort*, a little painting on copper by Guercino; *the Portrait of a Monk*, the *Bacchade* and the *Man with Monkey* are Annibale Carraci's works.

UFFIZI GALLERY. — « The Venus of the Medici ».

ROOM XXXVII — Dedicated to Rembrand. A Painting of the 17th century dominates this hall in its various aspects; the *Venus*, the *Prodigal Son* and the *Artemisia* are by Domenico Feti; the two canvases representing the *Parable of the Wedding Guest* and *Christ with the Pharisees* are by the Genovese Bernardo Strozzi. The Dutch painter Rembrandt shows us in this hall two *self-portraits* and a marvellous *Portrait of an old Man*. By another Dutch painter, Jacob Ruysdael, are the two landscapes exhibited on the last wall of the hall.

ROOM XXXVIII — 18th century room. Here are the following paintings of the Bolognese Giuseppe Maria Crespi, called the Spaniard: the *Poggio a Caiano Fair* and *Cupid and Psyche;* by Magnasco: *Four Scenes;* by Piazzetta, *Susannah and the Elders;* by Tiepolo, the canvas representing the *Erection of a Statue of an Emperor.* The two portraits are of the French painters Nicholas Largillière and Yacinthe Rigaud.

UFFIZI GALLERY. — Titian: « Venus of Urbino ».

Room XXXIX — Guardi Room. In this room some small paintings of Venetian artists of the 18th century are exhibited. Two pastels by Rosalba Carriera; two *portarits* by Alessandro Longhi; the *Confession* by Pietro Longhi; two *Views of Venice* by Canaletto (Antonio Canal); two *Views* by Guardi. The *portrait of the Countess of Grigna* by the French painter Mignard, and *Jesus* and *Saint John* by François Boucher.

UFFIZI GALLERY. — Titian: « Venus and Cupid ».

UFFIZI GALLERY. — Caravaggio: « Young Bacchus ».

Room XL — Crespi Room. The collection of the 18th century painters continues, among which are Crespi, Magnasco, Francesco de Mura, Giaquinto, Bernardo Bellotto with two *Views*, and Sebastiano Ricci with *Hercules and Cacus*.

Room XLI — Dedicated to Peter Paul Rubens. The great personality of this brilliant painter from Antwerp is here represented by the beautiful *Portrait of Isabelle Brandt* and the *Triumphal Entry of Henry IV into Paris*, opposite the *Triumphal Entry into Antwerp of Ferdinand of Austria*. The personal art of Anton van Dyk is represented by the *Portrait of Giovanni di Monfort*. The *Portrait of Galileo Galilei* is by Justus Sustermans. Various paintings are of the Rubens school.

Room XLII — In this Room, called the Niobe room, are exhibited the statues of *Niobe* and her *children* (the Niobidi) - Roman copies of original Greek models of the third and second centuries B.C. Provisionally exhibited here are the works of some 18th century French artists, Watteau, Nattier and Chardin.
For obvious reasons we are limiting our comments on each hall to the most important works.

THIRD ITINERARY

Piazza della Repubblica - Loggia del Mercato Nuovo (New Market) - Ponte Vecchio - Palazzo Pitti - Palatine Gallery - Boboli Gardens - Church of Santo Spirito - Church of Santa Maria del Carmine.

PIAZZA DELLA REPUBBLICA. — The modern centre of the town, stands on the site of the ancient Florence; demolished for hygenic reasons in the second half of the 17th century, to make way for the present piazza, which can be considered to be the most central and lively in the town. The huge triumphal arch joins the portico on one side, and under the arches of which the Central Post and Telegraph Office can be found.

VIA CALIMARA. — Going down this street; at the end càn be seen the Loggia del Mercato Nuovo a rinascimental work by Giovanni del Tasso (1547-51), which is completely open, with columns surmounted by arches. One time centre of the silk and gold trades, today it is extremely picturesque with its stalls selling straw goods and various articles made from lace, and is for this reason called the « Straw Market ». On the South side, there is the bronze statue of *a boar* by Pietro Tacca (1612), a reproduction of an antique statue which can be found in the Uffizi Gallery; the fountain is commonly called « del Porcellino », (of the little pig).

Behind the loggia of the Mercato Nuovo, in via di Carpaccio, there is the beautiful Palazzo di Parte Guelfa. Built at the beginning of the 14th century, it was altered and enlarged in the 15th by Brunelleschi who also began the facade, later completed by Giorgio Vasari. The latter also added the elegant little balcony. Inside on the first floor, there is a magnificent salon by Brunelleschi, with a wood ceiling by Vasari and a terracotta in the lunette by Luca della Robbia.

Following the side of the loggia we come to Via Porta Rossa. On turning left one can stop in Piazza Davanzati

Palazzo di Parte Guelfa.

Loggia del Mercato Nuovo (Straw Market).

and admire the PALAZZO DAVANZATI, a typical example of a 13th century private residence, and the TORRE DEI FORESI a characteristic tower-house, which is amongst the few remaining of the 150 that stood in Florence during the 13th century. They also provided a defence for the town.

VIA POR SANTA MARIA. — Returning up Via Porta Rossa, turning right and circling the Loggia di Mercato Nuovo (the straw Market), one enters Via Por Santa Maria, which was completely rebuilt after the last war. It is lined with numerous shops. Near the Ponte Vecchio, in a tiny piazza entered by a very narrow street, there is the romanesque Church of SANTO STEFANO AND SANTA CECILIA. Built in 1233 it has a facade decorated in green and white marble, so preserving its romanesque aspect. The interior was rebuilt in the 17th century by Pietro Tacca, and the building, partially damaged in the war, has been restored. Returning to Via Por Santa Maria, one can see, on the other side, two medieval tower-houses of the 11th and 13th centuries, and between them is that of the Amidei, so called the « Bigonciola », with two projecting *sculptures of lion's haeds*. At the end of the street one only need cross the narrow Lungarno to step on to the most famous bridge in the world.

Ponte Vecchio (Old Bridge).

PONTE VECCHIO

Thus named because it has existed from the time of the Etruscans and was reconstructed in the 14th century by Neri di Fioravanti. It is a picturesque construction with its lateral shops almost all kept by gold and silversmiths and, at the top on the left side the famous corridor by Vasari which puts the Uffizi Gallery in communication with the Pitti Palace. On the terrace of the bridge is a *bust of Benvenuto Cellini* by Raffaele Romanelli (1900).

VIA GUICCIARDINI. — After crossing Ponte Vecchio, we come to Via Guicciardini which has been completely reconstructed on top of the ruins left from the last war. In the little piazza on the left there stands the antique church of SANTA FELICITA. Built over a 5th century Oratory and Christian Burial ground, it has been reconstruc-

Pitti Palace.

ted many times. The present building of the 18th century, is by Ferdinando Ruggeri. Above the porch there is still the Vasarian passage which joins the Uffizi Gallery with Palazzo Pitti.

The interior is in the form of an Egyptian cross. In the first chapel on the right, which is by Brunelleschi, there is Pontormo's beautiful *Descent from the Cross* (1528). In the elegant sacresty; a work of one of Brunelleschi's followers (1470), there are some important paintings, amongst which are a *Madonna and Child with Saints;* a *polyptych* by Taddeo Gaddi, and *Santa Felicita and seven Children,* on a gold background, by Neri di Bicci. In the adjoining chapel, which has a hemispherical cupola, there is a *Crucifix* painted on wood, attributed to Pacino di Bonaguida, and a *Madonna and Child,* on wood, by Giovanni del Biondo. At the end of Via Guicciardini, on the left there is the PALAZZO GUICCIARDINI, built at the beginning of the 15th century, and partially altered in the 17th century. A few yards away is the vast Piazza Pitti, dominated by the huge mass of the Palazzo of the same name.

61

PITTI PALACE. — Bartolomeo Ammannati: The Courtyard.

PITTI PALACE

It is the most monumental of the Florentine palaces. It was built in the middle of the 15th century after the design of Filippo Brunelleschi, commissioned by Luca Pitti, an extremely rich merchant belonging to a family antagonistic to the Medici. He insisted on having a palace surpassing all of the others. In the following century the palace was widened at its two sides, and in the 17th century the lateral parts were also added, closing in the square and producing a suggestive effect both grandiose and solemn. The internal courtyard is by Ammannati (1558-70), who created an incomparable scenario dominated by the Artichoke Fountain in the Boboli gardens. Inside the Palace are the Palatine Gallery, the Silver Museum and the Gallery of Modern Art.

PALATINE GALLERY

The gallery, arranged in luxurious rooms, consists of 500 paintings, masterpieces of the greatest artists of every epoch, and in superb collections of precious objects which bear witness to the fabulous Medici wealth and the artistic traditon of this family who continued for generations to collect works of art and to give work to the great artists in all fields, showing such sensibility and enthusiasm that, because of them, Florence became that world centre of art, still today universally recognized and appreciated. The entrance to the gallery is to the left of the portico; entering by the gate leading to the Boboli gardens, one reaches the stairs leading to the entrance hall.

SALA DELLA ILIADE — (Iliad Room). The decorations in the ceiling are by Luigi Sabatelli (1819) with scenes of episodes from the Homeric Poem. The marble statue in the middle of the hall, *Charity* is by Lorenzo Bartolini (1824). On the walls: Raphael Sanzio: *Portrait of a Pregnant Woman* (1506). Andrea del Sarto: *Assumption of the Virgin* (1526). Ridolfo Ghirlandoio: *Female Portrait*. Baroccio: *Madonna and Saint Jerome*. Carlo Maratta: *Saint Philip Neri*. Sustermans: *Portrait of Count Waldemar Christian of Denmark*, considered to be his masterpiece. Diego Velasquez: *Equestian Portrait of Philip IV of Spain*.

SALA DI SATURNO — (Saturno Room). The decoration of the ceiling is the work of the Roman Ciro FERRI (1663-65), collaborator of Pietro da Cortona, to whom the drawings are attributed. In this hall several works by Raphael are exhibited, among them the famous: *Madonna della Seggiola* (Madonna of the Chair), one of his masterpieces also: the *Madonna del Granduca* (Madonna of the Grand-Duke), so called because il was the favorite painting of the Grand- Duke Ferdinando II, the *Madonna del Baldacchino*, an unfinished work executed during the last period of his stay in Florence, and the two famous *Portraits of Angelo and Maddalena Doni*, while the *Portrait of Tommaso Inghirami* and the *Portrait*

PALATINE GALLERY. — Iliad Room.

PITTI GALLERY. — Titian: « Portrait of a Lady ».

PITTI GALLERY. — Raphael: « Madonna of the Chair ».

Lorenzo Bartolini:
« The Charity ».

Sustermans: « Portrait of Count Waldemar Christian of Denmark »

of the Cardinal Dovizi da Bibbiena are attributed to him. The *Vision of Ezechiel* is supposed to be a drawing of Raphael, painted and completed by his pupil Giulio Romano. The *Descent from the Cross* and the *Magdalen* are by Perugino.

SALA DI GIOVE — (Jupiter Room). The Decorations in the ceiling are by Pietro da Cortona and Cirio Ferri. The statue in the middle of the hall, representing *Charity* is by Vincenzo Consani (1807). Andrea del Sarto has here one of his best works: *Saint John the Baptist*. Fra Bartolomeo: the *Descent from the Cross*. Rosso Fiorentino: *The Fates*. Peter Paul Rubens: *Nymphs pursued by Satyrs*. Andrea del Sarto: *Annunciation and Madonna in Glory*. Jacques Courtois, called the Borgognone: The *Battle*. Raphael: *The Veiled, Woman* (the « Fornarina »). Venetian School of the 16th century: the *Three Ages of Man*. Peter Paul Rubens: The *Holy Family*. Guercino: *Madonna of the Swallow*.

SALA DI MARTE — (Mars Room). The frescoes in the ceiling are by Pietro da Cortona and Ciro Ferri (1646). Bartolomeo E. Murillo: *Madonna with Child* and *Madonna of the Rosary*. Peter Paul Rubens: the *Four Philosophers* and the *Consequences of War*. Paolo Veronese: *Portrait of Daniele Barbaro*. Titian: *Portrait of the Cardinal Ippolito de' Medici* (1532), in Hungarian costume and the *Portrait of Andrea Vesalio*. Anton van Dyck: *Portrait of the Cardinal Bentivoglio*. Tintoretto: *Portrait of Luigi Cornaro*.

SALA DI APOLLO — (Apollo Room). Also in this hall the frescoes in the ceiling are by Pietro da Cortona and Ciro Ferri (1647-60). Titian is here represented by his two most beautiful works: the *Magdalen* and the *Portrait of a Gentleman with grey Eyes*. Tintoretto: *Portrait of Vincenzo Zeno*. Andrea del Sarto: the *Descent from the Cross* and the *Holy Family*. Van Dyck: *Portrait of Charles I of England and Henriette of France*.

SALA DI VENERE — (Venus Room). In the vault again are frescoes by Pietro Cortona and Cirio Ferri. The stuccoes by Roman artists (1642) are valuable. Very beautiful works by Titian are exhibited in this hall: *Portrait of a Woman, called « the Beautiful »*, the

Portrait of Pietro Aretino, the *Portrait of Giulio II* and the *Concert*, a work of his early years and very near to the style of Giorgione. The *Sacred Conservation* is by Bonifacio dei Pitati. The *Seascape* by Salvator Rosa.

From this hall we can pass into the Royal Apartments, but it is advisable to go first into the left hall in order to finish our visit of the Gallery.

SALA CASTAGNOLI — (Castagnoli Room), the name is derived from the painter of the frescoes (1851). In the middle of the room is a round table with *Apollo and the Muses* in hard precious stones. The *Saint Sebastian* is by Sodoma.

At the right we enter into the QUARTIERE DEL VOLTERRANO (Volterrano Apartment). The first room called of the *Allegories* contains works by Volterrano (Baldassarre Franceschini da Volterra), who also executed the decorations of the hall together with Giovanni da San Giovanni. The following room is called of the *Arts*, and contains works by C. Allori, Cigoli, Dolci, Ligozzi and Pietro Benvenuti. The fresco of the ceiling is by Podestà. The *Sèvres Vase* in the middle is a gift of Napoleon I to Ferdinando III. The following is the Sala dell'Aurora (Aurora Room) were works of Florentine painters of the 17th century are exhibited. The decorations of the vault are by G. Martellini.

We return to the Castagnoli Room and pass through the *Drum room* (Sala dei Tamburi), so called for the odd and original shape of the little tables, into the POCCETTI GALLERY deriving its name from the artist of the frescoes of allegoric figures in the vault. The works exhibited here are of the 17th century and belong to Francesco Furini: *Ila and the Nymphs*, lo Spagnoletto: *The Martyrdom of Saint Bartholomeo*, Poussin: *Landscapes*, Rubens: *Portrait of a Woman* and a *Self-portrait* by Salvator Rosa.

Fra Bartolomeo: « The Risen Christ among the Evangelist ».

Raphael: « Portrait of Cardinal Dovizi da Bibbiena ».

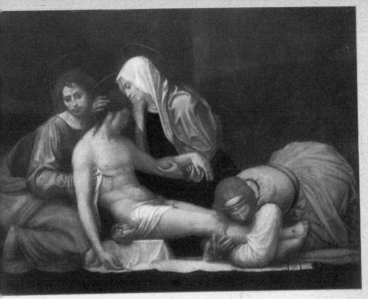

PALATINE GALLERY. — Fra Bartolomeo: « Deposition from Cross ».

SALA DI PROMETEO — (Prometheus Room). The decorations in the ceiling are by Collignon. The three very beautiful round pictures belong to Filippo Lippi: the *Madonna and Child*, Francesco Botticelli: the *Adoring Madonna*, and Luca Signorelli: the *Holy Family*. The *Portrait of a Woman* is by Botticelli; the *Holy Family* by Domenico Beccafumi and the *Dance of Apollo with the Muses* by Giulio Romano.

E. Murillo:
« Madonna and Child ».

E. Murillo:
« Madonna and Child ».

69

PITTI GALLERY. — Raphael: « Madonna of the Grand Duke ».

We enter to the right into the CORRIDOIO DELLE COLONNE (the corridor of the columns), where small pictures of Flemish and German schools are exhibited.

SALA-DELLA GIUSTIZIA — (Hall of Justice). The vault is decorated by Pio Fedi (1830) with the *Justice and Peace*. By Paolo Veronese, we see the *Baptism of Christ; Moses saved from the Waters* is by Bonifazio dei Pitati; the *Venus, Vulcan and Cupid* by Tintoretto; the *Portrait of Tommaso Mosti* and the *Image of the Saviour* are by Titian.

SALA DI FLORA (Flora Room). The frescoes in the vault are by Antonio Marini (1830). The *Venus*, in the middle of the hall, is by Antonio Canova. Important are the two paintings by Andrea del Sarto with *Stories of Joseph the Patriarch*. The *Adoration of the Magi* is by Pontormo; the *Portrait of Luca Martini* by Bronzino.

SALA DEI PUTTI — (Putti Room.) The frescoes in the vault are by Antonio Marini; In this hall paintings of Flemish and Dutch schools are exhibited: by Rachel Ruysch is the painting with *Flowers and Fruit;* by Hendrik G. Gubbels are the *Seascapes*. Returning to the Prometheus Room we pass into the

SALA DI ULISSE — (Ulysses Room). In the ceiling, *Return of Ulysses to Ithaca* is by Martellini. The painting of the *Madonna of the Window Pane* (Madonna dell'Impannata) (1514), is attributed to Raphael, but is thought to be painted by him and finished by his pupils. The grandiose painting representing the *Madonna and Child with Saints* is by Andrea del Sarto. The *portrait of Andrea Frizier* is by Tintoretto.

A small passage leading along the BATH ROOM (Sala da Bagno) is in neo-classical style.

SALA DELL'EDUCAZIONE DI GIOVE — (Education of Jupiter Room). The ceiling has been painted with frescoes by Luigi Catani. The *Sleeping Cupid* is by Caravaggio, the *Judith* by Cristoforo Allori. SALA DELLA STUFA — (The Stove Room). It is so called because it is at the sun side. The walls are painted all over with frescoes by Pietro da Cortona (1640) and the ceiling by Matteo Rosselli (1622).

Returning now to the Venus Room we enter from there into the

ROYAL APARTMENTS

In these halls too, which at one time were the residence of the kings of Italy, we shall limit ourselves to mention the most important works among the numerous ones decorating them.

DINING ROOM — (Sala da Pranzo) also called *of the Niches*. The various portraits of members of the Medici Family are by the painter of the court, Sustermans.

GREEN ROOM — (Sala Verde). Gobelin's Tapestries representing the *Stories of Esther* on drawings by François de Troy (1740).

THRONE ROOM — (Sala del Trono). Under the Baldachin we see the throne. The portraits are by Sustermans and by François Porbus. The Ceiling with *Jupiter between Juno and Minerva* is by Paolo Sarti.

BLUE ROOM — (Sala Celeste). Gobelin's tapestries and portraits by Sustermans. A beautiful Chinese vase is on the chimney mantelpiece.

PITTI PALACE — (ROYAL APARTMENTS). — Throne Room.

CHAPEL — (Cappella). Transformed into a drawing room after 1865. The altar is still visible behind the false wall. The portraits are by Sustermans.

PARROT ROOM — (Sala dei Pappagalli). So called for the parrots represented on tapestry. This hall, as well as the following ones, were the apartments at one time assigned to Queen Margherita. On the walls Gobelin's tapestry. The *Portrait of Giulia Varano, Duchess of Urbino* is by Titian and the *Portrait of Francesco I* is by Hans von Aachen.

SMALL ROOM AND BED ROOM — (Saletta e camera da letto). Gobelin's tapestry and *Portraits* by Sustermans and others. Return to the Parrot Room and, to the right, pass into the apartment of King Umberto I.

BED ROOM, STUDIO, DRAWING ROOM, ANTEROOM, BONA ROOM, decorated by Poccetti in the 17th century scenes representing: *Capture of the City of Bone in Africa; Capture of Prevesa in Albania;* the *Announcement of the Capture of Bone to Cosimo II;* the *Port of Leghorn.* In the ceiling: *Apotheosis of Cosimo I.*

WHITE HALL — (Sala Bianca). Also called *Ball Room.* The architecture is by Gaspare Maria Paoletti (XVIII century). The stuccoes and chandeliers are stupendous.

We have thus finished our visit of the Pitti Gallery.

MUSEUM OF PRECIOUS STONES

Going down the staircase to the ground floor, we come to the entrance of the Silver Museum.
The precious collections of this museum are derived, to a great extent, from the Medici Family and consist mainly of amber, ivories, gems, china ware, crystals and chattels.

ROOM I — Frescoes by Angiolo Michele Colonna and Agostino Mitelli (1644). Marble Busts on the walls. Opposite the windows, a

PITTI GALLERY. — Filippino Lippi: « Madonna and Child ».

most beautiful cabinet in ebony and precious stones of the
Elector Palatine, the last of the Medici Family, husband of Anna
Maria Luisa. In the central glass cases silver gilt cups by
Bavarian goldsmiths of the 16th and 17th centuries. On the
porphyry table, *Sleeping Children* by the Bernini school. At the
left, prié-dieu in ebony and mosaic. The great silver plate in the
corner represents *Madonna and the Mysteries of the Rosary*. The
bronze Crucifix is of the Giambologna school.

ROOM II — Decorated by the same artist as the previous one.
Interesting here are the *mosaics of birds' feathers*, mitre and
infulsa of Mexican art of the 16th century. In the other cases,
mainly works of Bavarian goldsmiths of the 16th and 17th
centuries.

P.P. RUBENS

PITTI GALLERY. — Peter Paul Rubens: « The Four Philosophers ».

ROOM III — The same decorators as the previous halls. The *cupboard chest of Alemagna*, in the middle, contains a little altar and little sacred statues in precious stones, belonging to the Cardinal Leopoldo, which served to celebrate the Holy Mass. After having passed through the corridor leading to the ROOM IV, at the left is the little Chapel with *Crucifix and Silver Chandeliers* executed by Bavarian goldsmiths.

ROOM IV — This is painted with frescoes by Giovanni da San Giovanni and his helpers. In the second glass case in the middle are *carved rock crystal cups and coveds in gold plate decorated with arabesques and enamelled* and precious work in semi-precious stones and blown glass of Florentine manufacture of the 16th century. In the third glass case, antique vases in amethyst and jasper belonging to Lorenzo de' Medici.

73

Room V — On the walls are tapestries of Florentine manufacture of the 16th and 17th centuries. In the glass cases, under the windows and opposite, precious pieces destined for the altar of the Chapel of the Princes, which however has never been completed; medallion in semi-precious stones, gold and brillants, executed by Orazio Moschini, designed by Giovanni Biliverti; *Seal of Cosimo I* engraved with emerald relief.

Room VI — Decoration of ceiling of the 17th century. Graceful little fountain of the 18th century. Here is a collection of cameos and carved jewels.
Returning to Room III we pass into

Room VII — Containing precious amber works.

Room VIII — We see materials, tapestries, embroideries, carpets and sacred objects. Of considerable importance are the embroidered *cope* and the « Paliotto » in embroidered silk, with silver, gold and precious stones representing the *Coronation of the Virgin and the Apostles*, work by Jacopo Cambi of the 14th century originating from the Church of Santa Maria Novella. By a staircase we ascend to a mezzanine floor where porcelain, materials and lace of high value are exhibited, which are of great interest. In the first room the *Portrait of Napoleon I* in Sèvres porcelain.
We go down again to the lower floor to end our visit in the rooms where ivory, mother of pearl, crystal and shell works are exhibited.

MODERN ART GALLERY

This contains works by XIX century, neoclassical, academic, and Macchiaioli artists. This last movement returned to art which, free of academic conventions, found the source of life and inspiration in direct contact with reality interpreted with an emotional and pictorical synthesis and manifested with sincerity of personal expression. At the head of the movement was Giovanni Fattori, with Silvestro Lega, Telemaco Signorini, Giuseppe Abbati, Raffaele Sernesi and others who are all represented here. There are also many works by contemporary and living artists.

BOBOLI GARDENS

It is a marvellous Italian garden, inspired by a precise structural concept. Niccolo Pericoli, called il Tribolo, conceived of the plan, commissioned by the Medici, and Ammannati and Buontalenti carried it out. In the 17th century the Island Piazzale, or square, was added. Entering the COURTYARD OF BACCHUS, with its fountain and the rather bizarre figure, we find at the end the GROTTO by Buontalenti, an imaginative ensemble of artificial grottes decorated with frescoes and sculptures. Taking the avenue to the right we reach the 17th century AMPHITHEATRE, with its central granite basin, coming from the Baths of Caracalla. From here we go to NEPTUNE'S FISH-POND and continuing left reach the BELVEDERE, from where we can enjoy a beautiful view of Florence and its hills. Going up to the statue of *Plenty*, by Giambologna, we reach on the right the KNIGHT'S GARDEN. Then we go down toward the FALCONING LAWN here the stupendous avenue leading to the ISLAND Piazzale begins; here there is the *Ocean Fountain* by Giambologna. From here, through the lemon grove, one can reach the exit and Via Romana.

VIA MAGGIO. — It is the most beautiful street on the other side of the Arno and is bordered by aristocratic palaces built during the XIV to XVII centuries. In the XVI century palace of the Buontalenti family, at No. 26, lived Bianca Cappello, Francesco de' Medici's mistress.

BOBOLI GARDENS. — Amphitheatre.

BOBOLI GARDENS. — Giambologna: « Fountain of the Ocean ».

SANTO SPIRITO

It is a church of the Augustinian order, conceived by Filippo Brunelleschi in 1444; Antonio Manetti and Salvi d'Andrea changed it considerably as they built it. The cupola, designed by Brunelleschi, was executed by Salvi d'Andrea; the graceful campanile is the work of Baccio d'Agnolo.

CHURCH OF THE CARMINE. — **Masaccio:** « St. Peter and St. John giving alms ».

The elegant interior with its light arches and its slender columns is in the form of a Latin Cross, with three naves with semi-circular chapel, once rich in works of art, which were subsequently transferred elsewhere. In the right transept, at the fifth altar, there are some works of

Filippino Lippi; at the seventh altar is the *sarcophagus of Neri Capponi* by Bernardo Rossellino; on the altars of the chapels in the apse are altar-pieces by Florentine artists of the 15th and 16th centuries. Worthy of note in the left transept: the *altar* sculpted in marble by Andrea Sansovino; the *wooden Crucifix*, attributed to the 20 year-old Michelangelo; the *Pietà* by Michelangelo, a copy of the original in Saint Peter's in Rome. The tabernacle on the main altar is by Giovanni Caccini (1608). The vestibule, with its barrel vault supported by 12 Corinthian columns, was built by Cronaca and precedes the sacresty, executed after the designs of Giuliano da Sangallo (1492).

SANTA MARIA DEL CARMINE

A church built at the end of the 13th century, it was destroyed by a fire in 1771 and re-built by Giuseppe Ruggeri and Giulio Mannaioni (1771-75) in the style of that were saved, together with the famous frescoes by Masaccio. The decoration of the Brancacci Chapel had been entrusted in 1422 to Masolino da Panicale, but when he was called to paint in Hungary the work was continued by Masaccio, who left here his great masterpiece, the Paying of the Tribute Money.

The frescoes in the Brancacci Chapel beginning on the left, are: above, 1) Masaccio: *Adam and Eve driven of Eden;* 2) Masaccio: *Paying of the Tribute Money;* 3) Masolino: *Saint Peter preaching a Sermon.* Below, on the left; 4) Filippino Lippi: *Saint Paul visiting Saint Peter in Prison;* 5) the right side of the fresco, with *Saint Peter on his Thron*, is by Masaccio, while the left side, with *Saint Peter reviving the Nephew of the Emperor*, was begun by Masaccio, and completed by Filippino Lippi; 6) Masaccio: *Saint Peter healing the Sick.* On the right side of the altar, above: 1) Masaccio: *Saint Peter baptising the Neophytes;* 2) on the left, Masaccio: *Saint Peter heals the Lame Man;* on the right, Masolino: *the Resurrection of Tabitha;* 3) Masolino: the *Temptation of Abraham;* 4) Masaccio: *Saint Peter and Saint John giving Alms;* 5) Filippino Lippi: the *Condemnation and Crucifixion of Saint Peter;* 6) Filippino Lippi: *the Angel freeing Saint Peter from Prison.*

FOURTH ITINERARY

Piazza del Duomo - Via Tornabuoni - Palazzo Strozzi - Church of Santa Trinita - Lungarno Corsini - Church of Santa Maria Novella.

VIA CERRETANI. — One of the more animated streets of the town, it joins Piazza del Duomo with the Central Station. On the left can be seen the side of the church of SANTA MARIA MAGGIORE; whose entrance is in the piazza of the same name. This is a very old church which stood inside the walls of the city. It was re-built at the end of the XIII century, but traces of the X century romanesque construction can still be seen. Over the porch-way there is a *Madonna and Child;* a XIV century work of the Pisan School. The interior, with three vaulted naves, contains the tomb of Dante's master Bruno Latini, and the remains of XIV century frescoes. In the left chapel of the presbytery is a painted relief on wood, of the *Madonna Enthroned with the Child*, attributed to Coppo di Marcovaldo. - Following Via Cerretani, one soon comes to the central office of the C.I.T., situated on the corner. After turning left and taking the short Via Rondinelli, one arrives in Piazza Antinori.

PIAZZA ANTINORI. — This takes its name from the XV century PALAZZO DEGLI ANTINORI which stands on the right of the square. The building is attributed to Giuliano da Maiano. Almost in front of this is the church of SAN GAETANO, originally romanesque, but completely re-built in 1648 in the Florentine Baroque style, by Matteo Nigetti, and Gherardo and Pier Francesco Silvani.

VIA TORNABUONI. — This is the most aristocratic street of Florence, and is said to be one of the most beautiful in the world. It is lined by magnificent buildings, antique-shops and bookshops, etc. On the right at N°. 19

Palazzo Strozzi.

Palazzo Antinori.

stands the Palazzo Lardarel, an elegant late-renaissance structure by Giovanni Antonio Dosio (1580), on the left, at N°. 20, Palazzo Corsi, which was altered in the XIX century and has a beautiful courtyard by Michelozzo; at N°. 15 Palazzo Viviani già Della Robbia, where the famous family of artists lived, and which was altered in 1639 by G.B. Foggini. We now arrive at a cross-road: on the left is Via Strozzi, an elegant and lively street which leads to Piazza della Repubblica; to the right there are two streets; Via della Spada and Via della Vigna Nuova. The latter leads to Piazza Rucellai, where, on the left, one can see the three arches of the Loggia dei Rucellai, attributed to Leon Battista Alberti (1460). The wall was added in the XVII century. On the left stands the beautiful Palazzo Rucellai, masterpiece of early renaissance architecture, built by Bernardino Rossellino from the design by Leon Battista Alberti (1446-51) and which differs from the other XV century Florentine palaces: it has three floors and the facade is in smooth-hewn stone, is intersperced with elegant cornices, pillars and large triple windows of traditional design. The pleasant courtyard, later altered, is probably by Rossellino. The custodian of the palace will accompany visitors to the restored Rucellai Chapel, which is entered from Via della Spada. This street contains the *tabernacle of Holy Sepulchre,* a little rectangular temple of polichrome

80

marble by Leon Battista Alberti, and commissioned by Giovanni di Paolo Rucellai. Turning back up Via della Vigna Nuova, one returns into Via Tornabuoni; where the Palazzo Strozzi stands.

PALAZZO STROZZI

This is one of the most beautiful examples of Florentine renaissance palaces. It was begun by Benedetto da Maiano ih 1489, commissioned by Filippo Strozzi; the rich merchant and rival of the Medici family, who sent him into exile, where he increased his riches. The palace was then continued by Cronaca (Simone del Pollaiolo), who worked on it from 1497-1507, leaving it incomplete however. The elegant building in rusticated stone has two rows of double mullioned windows and a magnificent cornice. The wrought-iron lanterns and heavy iron rings àre by Nicolò Grosso, nicknamed « il caparra » (the deposit), because of his eccentric character. He never carried out work; commissioned by prince or ordinary citizen if it was not anticipated by a deposit. The superb internal courtyard, in the form of a portico, has two rows of loggias, and is by Cronaca.

Continuing along Via Tornabuoni; on the left is PALAZZO ALTOVITI, surmounted by a loggia, and joined in 1827 by the architect Silvestri to PALAZZO SANGALLETTI. On the right at No. 5 is PALAZZO MINERBETTI (XIV century). One then comes to piazza Santa Trinita.

PIAZZA SANTA TRINITA. — In the centre of this Piazza is the Roman granite column from the Terme di Caracalla, given to Cosimo I by Pio IV (1560), it is surmounted by the porphyry *statue of Justice*, by Francesco Ferrucci the younger, called Tadda (1581). On the left, at No. 2 is PALAZZO BARTOLINI SALIMBENI, whose facade has two rows of mullioned windows and niches by Baccio d'Agnolo (1520-29). Further on again, to the left, on the corner of the piazza, one comes to Borgo SS. Apostoli, one of the most characteristic medieval streets of Florence, bordered by houses and towers of the XIII to XIV centuries. Past these, one soon finds oneself in the piazza surrounding the church of SS. Apostoli, which was built in the XI century and later restored. In the facade is an elegant XVI century porch-

way, attributed to Benedetto da Rovezzano. The interior
has three naves divided by columns and preserves its
primitive structure. It contains valuable works of art:
On the left side of the presbytery the *sepulchre of Bindo
Altoviti* can be found above the sacresty door, and above
that, the *statue of Charity*, attributed to Ammannati. On
the left of the *High Altar* are the tabernacle in glazed
terracotta by Andrea Della Robbia, and the *sepulchre of
Oddo Altoviti*, by Benedetto da Rovezzano. The church
also contains the stone with which the sacred fire is
lighted on Easter Saturday, and that, according to the
legend, was brought from the Holy Land by the crusader
Pazzino de' Pazzi. - Returning to piazza Santa Trinita, on
one's immediate right is the battlemented PALAZZO SPINI -
FERRONI, an austere XIII century construction, which
maintains its fortress-like character. Opposite stands the
elegant PALAZZO GIANFIGLIAZZI, which is also of the XIII
century, and on whose right is the facade of the church
of Santa Trinita.

CHURCH OF SANTA TRINITÀ

Built by the Vallombrosian monks in the 11th century,
it was enlarged in the 13th century. The facade is by
Bernardo Buontalenti (1593).

The interior is divided into three Gothic naves. Inside
there are important works by artists of the 14th and 15th
centuries, among which, on the altar in the third chapel,
the *Madonna with Child and Saints* by Neri di Bicci; in
the fourth chapel, frescoes by Lorenzo Monaco with
Scenes from the Life of the Virgin and the *Annunciation*,
panel on the altar. In the fifth chapel the beautiful *marble
altar* is by Benedetto da Rovezzano. The SASSETTI
CHAPEL, first in the right transept, is an important one,
being entirely covered with frescoes by Domenico Ghirlandaio (1486), and containing the *tomb* of the Sassetti
family by Giuliano da Sangallo. On the altar in the main
chapel the *polyptych* is by Marioto di Nardo (1416). In
the next chapel, the *tomb* of Benozzo Federici, done in
marble by Luca della Robbia. In the fifth chapel on the
left there is a statue of *Mary Magdalen* by Desiderio da
Settignano (1464), and completed by Benedetto da Maiano
(1468); in the following chapel, the *tomb of Dino Com-
pagni* (1250-1324), a chronicler of the time of Dante. In

the next chapel the altar panel by Neri di Bicci, of the *Annunciation,* and a *Roman sarcophagus* in which Giuliano Davanzati is buried.

On leaving the church and turning right towards the Arno, at the end of the street one finds SANTA TRINITA BRIDGE.

PONTE SANTA TRINITA. — It is the most majestic of the Arno's bridges. Constructed in 1252 by the architects fra Sisto and fra Ristoro, it was later reconstructed, between 1566 and 1569, by Bartolommeo Ammannati, influenced by Michelangelo, creating one of the most beautiful Italian Rinascimental bridges. It has three arches, supported by powerful pillars, and the *statues of the four seasons* were added in 1608. It was completely destroyed by German mines on the night of 4th August, 1944, and has been faithfully reconstructed « where it was and as it was », largely using the remains of the old construction (1955-57).

LUNGARNO CORSINI. — On turning left one goes along the most beautiful part of the riverside road, which takes its name from the Corsini family, in whose number were personages of historical importance, such as Lorenzo Corsini, who became Pope Clemente XII (XVIII century) and Andrea Corsini, Bishop of Fiesole. The road is bordered by magnificent buildings: at No. 2, now the British Consulate, is the PALAZZO GIANFIGLIAZZI, which was altered in the XIX century simultaneously with the rinascimental building next to it, which is also of the Gianfigliazzi family. At No. 10 is the PALAZZO CORSINI, built by P. Silvani and E. Ferri (1648-56), it consists of a central structure with two lateral wings. These are terraced and adorned with statues. It is amongst the best examples of Florentine Baroque. On the first floor is the CORSINI GALLERY, one of the most important private art collections in Italy.

PIAZZA OGNISSANTI. — Bordered by large hotels, it has in the centre a modern sculpture of *Hercules killing the lion,* by Romanelli. The facade of the church of OGNISSANTI provides a background to the piazza. It was built in the XIII century and altered in the XVII century. In the lunette above the door there is glazed terracotta of the *Crowning of the Virgin* by Benedetto Buglioni. The elegant campanile is the original construction of the XIII century. The interior, with one nave and a transept, contains valuable works of art: under the second altar

Church of Santa Maria Novella.

on the left; frescoes by Domenico and Davide Ghirlandaio of about 1470, and above them a *tombstone* to the Vespucci family; between the third and fourth altars; a magnificent fresco depicting *Sant'Agostino in his study*, by Botticelli (1480). In the chapel of the right arm of the transept; a small disc indicates where the mortal remains of Botticelli lie. The frescoes in the cupola are by Giovanni da San Giovanni (1617). Between the third and fourth altars of the left side there is the *fresco of San Girolamo in his study,* by Domenico Ghirlandaio (1480). To the of left of the church one can enter the rinascimental CLOISTER; and from here into the refectory of the convent, on whose wall there is the famous LAST SUPPER BY DOMENICO GHIRLANDAIO, which he painted in 1480.

Turning left and going up Borgo Ognissanti, where, in Piazza Goldoni, one must turn into Via dei Fossi, which leads up to Piazza Santa Maria Novella.

PIAZZA SANTA MARIA NOVELLA. — This is one of the most beautiful and grandiose squares of Florence, dominated by the marble facade of the church which gives it its name. On the left side is the elegant XV century LOGGIA DI SAN PAOLO, which is decorated with medallions in terracotta by Giovanni Della Robbia; under the portico is the beautiful lunette by Andrea Della Robbia depicting *San Domenico and San Francesco meeting*. The two *obelisks* surmounted by bronze lilies and standing on bronze tortoises are by Giambologna (1608) and were erected to divide the piazza for the famous « Palio dei Cocchi », a chariot race of Roman inspiration, begun by Cosimo I in 1563.

CHURCH OF SANTA MARIA NOVELLA

A church belonging to the Dominical order, it was built by two Dominicans, Fra' Sisto da Firenze and Fra' Ristoro da Campi; later it must have been finished by another monk of the same order, Jacopo Talenti, who also built the extraordinarily agile Gothic-Romanesque campanile. It is the first church of monumental proportions built in Florence. The white and green marble decorations were definitively completed in 1470. The upper part of the facade and the central doorway are Renaissance in character, and we see that from several styles happily combined, a new source of harmony is born. To the right and left of the facade are Gothic tombs, belonging to illustrious Florentine families.

THE INTERIOR is a T-shaped cross, with three naves delineated by pilasters and vaulted naves. In the right nave the *monument of the Blessed Villana* by Bernardo Rossellino (1451) is worthy of note, and, in the right transept in a corner, over the *bust of Saint Antonino*, Archbishop of Florence is the *tomb of Tedice Aliotti*, Bishop of Fiesole, by Tino da Camaino. At the end of the transept is the RUCELLAI CHAPEL where was the Madonna of Duccio di Boninsegna, now in the Uffizi. Following are the CHAPEL OF THE SACRAMENT with remains of frescoes by the school of Giotto; the CHAPEL OF FILIPPO STROZZI, with frescoes by Filippino Lippi (1502) and the *tomb of Filippino Strozzi* by Benedetto da Maiano (1491); the CHAPEL OF THE MAIN ALTAR with the *tomb of Leonardo Dati* by Ghiberti (1423), the frescoes by

Domenico Ghirlandaio and assistants (1486-90) which cover the walls and the vault of the apse. In the left transept; the GONDI CHAPEL with remains of frescoes by Greek painters of the 13th century and the famous *polychrome wood Crucifix* by Filippo Brunelleschi; the Gaddi Chapel with the *Miracle of Christ*, a panel by Agnolo Bronzino; the STROZZI OF MANTOVA CHAPEL, which delimits the transept, with frescoes by Nardo di Cione Arcagnolo and his brother Andrea, both called Orcagna, representing the *Last Judgement, Hell and Paradise* according to the Dantesque conception. On the altar is a beautiful panel by Andrea Orcagna with *Christ triumphant* (1357). In the sacristy, by Jacopo Talenti (1350), is a large painted *Crucifix* attributed to Giotto, and a terracotta basin by Giovanni della Robbia (1498). In the left nave is the very important fresco by Masaccio of the *Holy Trinity*, one of the last works of the master, of accentuated and airy perspective and great humanity. The pulpit near the second to the last pilaster was executed from the design by Brunelleschi and completed by his pupil Andrea Cavalcanti, called il Buggiano. On the wall at the end, on the top lunette, is a mosaic of the *Nativity* from a cartoon of the school of Filippino Lippi; below, to the right, *Annunciation, Nativity, Baptism*, and *Adoration*, of the school of Giotto, attributed to Agnolo Gaddi.

CLOISTER OF SANTA MARIA NOVELLA. — The cloisters are to the left of the church, and the first one is the GREEN CLOISTER built in approximately 1350 by Fra' Giovanni da Campi; it is Romanesque in style. It is thus named after the colour of the frescoes, it once had been painted by Paolo Uccello in the 14th century. The famous frescoes of the *Flood* and *Scenes from the Life of Noah* are kept in a room of the refectory. The SPANISH CHAPEL is in the cloister, built by Jacopo Talenti in 1359 in honor of Saint Thomas Aquinas and decorated with frescoes by Andreo Buonaiuto (1366-68), called Andrea da Firenze. The paintings are of: the *Triumph of Saint Thomas Aquinas* the Church Militant. Scenes from the New Testament. On the wall: *Scenes from the Passion and*, on the entrance wall, *Scenes from the Life of Saint Peter, Martyr*.

ELONGAVI FVGIENS 7 MANSI INSOLITVDINE . PS . XXXXXV . C

SVRGE ACCIPE PVERVM 7 MATREM EP 7 FVGE INEGIPTVM . MACEI . II . C

MUSEUM OF SAN MARCO. — **Beato Angelico**: « The Fligt into Egypt ».

FIFTH ITINERARY

Piazza del Duomo - Church of San Marco - Museum of San Marco - Gallery of the Academy - Church of SS. Annunziata - Archaeological Museum.

MUSEUM OF SAN MARCO. — **Beato Angelico**: « Deposition ».

PIAZZA SAN MARCO. — This can be reached by going along the first part of Via Cavour, which is the continuation of Via Martelli. In its centre is the monument to General Manfredo Fanti, by Pio Fedi (1873), and bordering it are the church of San Marco with the adjoining convent containing the San Marco Museum; the University and, on the corner of Via Ricasoli, the XIV century portico of the ACADEMY OF FINE ARTS, which was once part of the OSPEDALE DI SAN MATTEO: under the portico, in the lunette, are Robbian terracottas. At N. 60, Via Ricasoli there is the Galleria dell'Accademia (Gallery of the Academy) and the tribune of David.

CHURCH OF SAN MARCO

A 13th century church, later restored by Michelozzo in 1437, by Giambologna in 1580 and finally by Pier Francesco Silvani in 1678, who is responsible for its present appearance.
Inside there are works by painters and sculptors of the 15th and 16th century. In the sacristy, by Michelozzo, a sarcophagus with the reclining statue of *Saint Antonino*, the Archbishop of Florence. The body of the Saint is in the left transept, under the altar of the CHAPEL OF SAINT ANTONINO, designed by Giambologna.

MUSEUM OF SAN MARCO. — **Michelozzo:** Cloister of St. Antonino.

MUSEUM OF SAN MARCO

The museum is in the convent of San Marco, commissioned by Cosimo il Vecchio to Michelozzo, for the use of the Dominican friars of Fiesole. Among them there was a Fra' Giovanni da Fiesole, a painter called Fra' Angelico because of the sweetness of his angelic figures. Fra' Girolamo Savonarola also lived in this convent from 1489 to 1498.

Entering the cloister, called the Cloister of Saint Antonino, one passes by a series of frescoes showing *episodes from the life of the Saint*. Opposite is the very beautiful *Crucifix with Saint Dominic*, by Fra' Angelico and the two painted lunettes with *Saint Peter Martyr and Saint Thomas Aquinas*. Passing into a room of the CHAPTER HOUSE we see the great dramatic, and yet seraphic composition of the *Crucifix* by Fra' Angelico. On the other side of the cloister is the PILGRIMS' HOSPICE ROOM which contains pannel paintings of Fra' Angelico: because of the sweetness of his angelic figures. Fra' Girolamo Savonarola also lived in this convent from 1489 to 1498.

Entering the cloister, called the Cloister of Saint Antonino, one passes by a series of frescoes showing *episodes from the life of the Saint*. Opposite is the very beautiful *Crucifix with Saint Dominic,* by Fra' Angelico and the two painted lunettes with *Saint Peter Martyr and Saint Thomas Aquinas.* Passing into a room of the CHAPEL HOUSE we see the great dramatic, and yet seraphic, composition of the *Crucifix* by Fra' Angelico. On the other side of the cloister is the PILGRIMS' HOSPICE ROOM which contains panel paintings of Fra' Angelico: extraordinary is the tabernacle of the *Madonna of the Linaioli* (flax-workers), very beautiful is the *Coronation of the Virgin,* and stupendous is the *Last Judgement, among* other works, all of which have the purpose of glorifying the faith. On the second floor there is the admirable fresco of the *Annunciation,* of a profound mysticism; to the left, *Saint Dominic adoring the Crucifix.* Each cell at either side of the corridor has a fresco by Fra' Angelico or by a student working on a design of his master. In cell 1, the *Noli me tangere;* cell 3 the *Annunciation;* cell 4 the *Crucifixion;* cell 6 the *Transfiguration;* cell 7 *Christ derided;* celle 9 the *Crowning of Mary;* cell 11, *Madonna with Child and Saints.* At the end of the corridor are the PRIOR'S APPARTMENTS, composed of three cells, where Fra' Girolamo Savonarola lived; he attempted to reform the morals of his time and was burned at the stake. On the 8th of April 1498, he was removed from this convent for the execution of his penalty. The *portrait of Savonarola* is by Fra' Bartolomeo. The cells near the left wall have frescoes of *Crucifixes* by pupils of Fra' Angelico. In the 31st cell, which once belonged to Saint Antonino, there are *relics of the Bishop* and a *funeral mask.* Cell 38 and 39 were reserved for Cosimo de' Medici when he withdrew here to meditate. The *portrait of Cosimo de' Medici* is attributed to Pontormo. In the LIBRARY, by Michelozzo (1441), illuminated hymnals of the 14th and 15th centuries. On the ground floor, in the refectory, there is a fresco of the *Last Supper* by Domenico Ghirlandaio. In the large cloister, called the CLOISTER of SAINT DOMINIC, by Michelozzo, are some remnants of old Florence.

GALLERY OF THE ACADEMY. → The Vestibule and the Tribune of David.

GALLERY OF THE ACADEMY

Contains sculptures by Michelangelo and paintings of the Tuscan school from the 13th to the 16th century. VESTIBULE: walls decorated with Flemish and Florentine tapestries of the 16th, 17th and 18th centuries. Near

Detail of the Adimari Chest (15th century).

GALLERY OF THE ACADEMY. — Michelangelo: « David ».

the walls are two rough casts of *Prisoners*, by Michelangelo, which together with those in the Louvre in Paris were intended for the tomb of Julius II, planned by Michelangelo. In the Tribune, the work of Emilio de Fabris (1882), the famous *David* is enthroned, sculpted by Michelangelo at the age of 25 (1501-4). In the other rooms are gathered paintings of the Tuscan School from the 13th to the 16th century: Bernardo Daddi, Agnolo Gaddi, Giovanni da Milano, Giovanni del Biondo, Taddeo Gaddi, (worthy of note the *Scenes from the Life of Christ and Saint Francis*, Spinello Aretino, Lorenzo Monaco, Filippino Lippi, Sandro Botticelli, Paolo Uccello and others. One can see in the gallery two original plaster models by Giambologna for the *Rape of the Sabine Women* and the *group of the Victory*.

CENACOLO DI SANT'APOLLONIA. — (Last Supper by Andrea del Castagno). (Entrance Via XVII Aprile 1). This and other frescoes, painted in 1450-57, can be found in the refectory of the Benedictine convent of Sant'Apollonia. Apart from the *Last Supper,* a work of intense realism, there are, by the same artist: *The Crucifixion, The Deposition; Resurrection,* and on the other walls: *Crucifixion and Saints; Pietà* and the famous cycle of illustrious persons taken from the Villa Pandolfini at Legnaia: Boccaccio, Petrarch, Dante, Queen Tamaris, Queen Esther, the sibly of Cuma, Niccolò Acciaiuli, Farinata degli Uberti and Pippo Spano.

CHIOSTRO DELLO SCALZO. — Via Cavour 69. It is so called because the cross-bearer of the religious brotherhood of the Scalzo always walked barefoot in processions. It is a little porticoed courtyard, built at the beginning of the XVI century, with frescoes in chiaroscuro, depicting stories in the *life of St. John the Baptist,* by Andrea del Sarto and Franciabigio (1514-26).

PIAZZA SANTISSIMA ANNUNZIATA. — The Florentine square which wholly contains the harmony of the Renaissance spirit, the perfect balance of dimensions and the serene sense of proportion which Florence, through its buildings and other works, contributed to the Renaissance: a square which can be truly appreciated in its real beauty when there are no cars or other vehicles, and it is completely empty. Opposite is the Church of the Santissima Annunziata; to the right, the portico of the Ospedale degli Innocenti, completed by Brunelleschi in the years between 1421 and 1424. In the spaces of the arcades the medallions with figures of putti in various attitudes are in glazed terracotta, the work of Andrea della Robbia. Opposite is the portico of the CONFRATERNITA' OF THE SERVI DI MARIA, by Antonio da Sangallo and Baccio d'Agnolo (1525). In the centre of the square is an *equestrian statue of the Grand Duke Ferdinand I* by Giambologna and Pietro Tacca (1608). The two bronze fountains, with figures of marine monsters, are the work of Tacca and his assistant.

INNOCENTI GALLERY. — We enter through the portico to the right of the square.

At the end of the courtyard there is a glazed terracotta depicting the *Annunciation* by Andrea della Robbia. The gallery contains various works, amongst which is the magnificent *Adoration of the Magi* by Domenico Ghirlandaio, which he painted for the church of the hospital. The other paintings are by Giovanni del Biondo, Piero di Cosimo, and Neri di Bicci, whilst the sculptures are by Luca Della Robbia.

CHURCH OF SANTISSIMA ANNUNZIATA

The church was built in approximately 1250 by the founders of the Order of the Servi di Maria, but in the middle of the 15th century it was reconstructed, and in the 17th and 18th centuries underwent substantial alterations, thereby acquiring its present appearance. From the portico, begun by Antonio Sangallo and finished by Giovanni Caccini (1621), one can enter the ATRIUM, called the Cloister of Vows, built by Antonio Manetti (1457), on the design by Michelozzo. The frescoes in the lunettes under the portico are interesting, they were done by G. B. Rosso, Pontormo, Franciabigio, Andrea del Sarto, A. Baldovinetti and C. Rosselli.

THE INTERIOR, which has a single nave with lateral chapels, is richly decorated in the Baroque style The ceiling is inlaid with decorated stuccoes. To the left there is the small marble TEMPLE OF THE ANNUNZIATA, by Lapo

Portigiani after the design by Michelozzo. First chapel on the left, *Saint Julian* by Andrea del Castagno; second chapel, frescoes by Andrea del Castagno; fourth chapel, *Assumption* by Perugino. THE CRUCIFIX CHAPEL, in the left transept, contains a *Saint John the Baptist*, terracotta statue by Michelozzo. Rotunda: the frescoes in the cupola with the *Crowning of the Virgin*, are by Volterrano; to the left is the *tomb of the Bishop Angelo Marzi Medici*, by Francesco da Sangallo (1546); on the floor, is a *stone commemorating Andrea del Sarto*. Behind the Choir is the CAPPELLA DEL SOCCORSO, arranged by Giambologna to contain his tomb and those of Flemish artists who died in Florence. The *Crucifix* on the altar and the bronze bas-reliefs with *Scenes from the Passion*, are by Giambologna. In the chapel to the left of this the *Resurrection* is by Agnolo Bronzino and the wooden *statue of Saint Rocco* by the Nuremberg sculptor, Viet Stoss. To the right of the Rotunda is the *tomb of Donato dell'Antella* by G. B. Foggini. In the first chapel in the right transept, the marble *Deposition* is by Baccio Bandinelli, buried here in 1559.

ARCHAEOLOGICAL MUSEUM

(Entrance N. 9 Piazza SS. Annunziata, on the corner of Via della Colonna). This is housed in Palazzo della Crocetta, and is one of the biggest and most interesting in Italy. It is composed of three sections: The Topographical Museum of Etruria, The Egyptian Museum and the Etrusco and Greco-Roman Museum.

On the ground floor, the first rooms contain greco-roman sculpture, amongst which, of particular interest are: *Little satyr looking at his tail*, a copy of the bronze original. II century B.C.; *Satyr with child Dionysus* (Bacchus) a Roman copy of the bronze of the Hellenistic age; Large statue of *Aphrodite;* Large statue of *Caryatid;* Small fragmentary statue of *Artemis*, copy of a Greek original of the V century B.C.; *Apollo* and the *Milani Apollo;* sculptures of the VI and V centuries B.C.; *The Lion of Val Vidone*, in a rough grey stone called « Nenfro ». Etruscan work of the IV-III centuries B.C. - Following these rooms are those of the TOPOGRAPHICAL MUSEUM OF ETRURIA, which contain archeological objectes, from identified places, representing all the

Etruscan peoples. It is arranged topographically in the various Etruscan centres and their evolution from VIII-I century B.C. Notices outside all the rooms list the various objects displayed and their origin. The most important centres represented: TARQUINIA (rooms 12-14), where the objects of particular interest are: biconical urns with lids in the shape of crested or cup-shaped helmets; some in earthenware and some in bronze, sarcophagus in nenfro of the IV century B.C. - TUSCANIA (rooms 15 and 16), earthenware sarcophagi of the III-II centuries B.C. ORVIETO (room 18), *funerary Head of a Warrior*, in nenfro, of the V century B.C. - VULCI (room 19), *Funerary Lion in nenfro*, V century B.C. - VETULONIA (rooms 25-28) objects from tombs of the VII-VI centuries B.C. - POPULONIA (rooms 29-31) bronze clasp with tiny *Venus resembling the Medici Venus*. - CLUSIUM (rooms 39-46). Funerary statue of a mother and child, known as the « *Mater Matuta* », the *mother goddess of the Etruscans*, V century B.C. - LUNI (rooms 49) Decorative pediments from two temples dedicated to the *Capitoline Triad*, and *Apollo and Diana*, II century B.C.

In the garden there are tombs and monuments reconstructed with the original materials, particularly Etruscan. Rooms 50-51 are dedicated to the prehistoric section.

EGYPTIAN MUSEUM. — This consists of objects discovered by the Tuscan Expedition led by Ippolito Rossellini, which in 1828-9 carried out excavations in Egypt, in collaboration with a French expedition led by Champollion. In the eight rooms of the first floor are sculptures, sarcophagi, mummies, gold objects; papyruses, etc., and of particular interest are: the *Goddess Hathor in the guise of a cow, suckling Pharoah Herenheb* (XIV century B.C.); *red basalt bust of pharoah;* (XVIII century B.C.); *Coloured relief of the Goddess Hathor extending her hand to Pharoah Sethos* (XIII century B.C.); two coloured *statues in wood of two serving-maids,* one kneading paste for beer, and the other kneading flour (2625-2475 B.C.); ancient chariot found in a tomb in the necropolis of Thebes, XIV century B.C.

ETRUSCO AND GRECO-ROMAN SECTION. — This contains objects that were part of the Medici and Lorena collections, added to with gifts and purchases. Of exceptional interest are the *sarcophagus of Ramta Uzenai*, IV century B.C.; *Minerva of Arezzo* in the style of Praxiteles, a copy

ARCHAEOLOGICAL MUSEUM. — « The Chimaeres of Arezzo ».

made by an Etruscan artist; *Chimaeres of Arezzo*, Etruscan art of the IV century B.C.; *Orator* (l'Arringatore) statue in honour of Aulus Metellus the Etruscan, III-II century B.C.; *The Idolino*, a Greek original of the V century B.C.; *Horse's head*, of the Hellenistic age, which probably gave Donatello inspiration for the horse in the Gattamelata statue at Padua. - On the same floor are collections of ancient money, gems; cameos; silver, etc. - On the second floor the Etruscan and Greco-Roman Section continues. There is archaeological material from North and South Italy, and from Cyprus, Crete, Greece and Rhodes, and attic vases with black figures, of the VI century B.C., amongst which is the famous *François vase*, signed by the potter Ergotimos and the painter Klitias. The design show Greek mythological scenes with black figures on a red ground; Etruscan terracottas; frescoes detached from Etruscan tombs; reproductions of Etruscan paintings from the tombs at Vulci, Tarquinia and Clusium and a coloured *sarcophagus of Larthis Seianti*, of the V centuries B.C.

SANTA MARIA MADDALENA DE' PAZZI. — Via della Colonna 7. In the Chapter House is the famous *Fresco by Perugino* (1493-96), depicting the *Crucifixion with the Magdalene at the foot of the Cross*. On the left: *St. Bernard and the Virgin*, and on the right: *St. John and St. Benedict*.

Piazza San Firenze.

SIXTH ITINERARY

Piazza del Duomo - National Museum (Bargello) - Church of the Badia - Buonarroti House - Piazza and Church of Santa Croce - Horne Museum - Bardini Museum.

VIA DEL PROCONSOLO. — This street begins to the left of the external part of the apse of the Cathedral, and is one of the oldest in Florence. A little way further on there is the small Piazza di Santa Maria del Campo, where there is the church of the same name. Past the

    NATIONAL MUSEUM. — Michelangelo: « Martyrdom of St. Andrew » (detail).

NATIONAL MUSEUM. — Michelangelo: « Bust of Brutus ».

piazza, at No. 12 on the corner of Borgo degli Albizi, there is the PALAZZO NONFINITO (unfinished), begun in 1539 by Bernardo Buontalenti, commissioned by Alessandro Strozzi, then continued by G. B. Caccini, Matteo Nigetti and others, but never finished. At present it houses the MUSEUM OF ANTRHOPOLOGY AND ETHNOLOGY, founded in 869 by Paolo Mantegazza, which contains collections relative to the various human races, to prehistory and to African Asiatic, Indonesian and American civilisations. On the other corner, at No. 10 there is the rinascimental PALAZZO PAZZI-QUARATESI, which has two floors and splendid triple windows. It was built for the Pazzi family by Giuliano da Maiano (1462-72). Further on, to the left, is Via Dante Alighieri which leads to a very picturesque corner of Florence, where the Alighieri Family's houses once stood. On the corner is the so-called HOUSE OF DANTE, which has been restored; and where it is said the great poet was born. Continuing along Via del Proconsolo, on the right is the Badia Church, and further on, to the left, is the Palazzo del Bargello, which contains the National Museum. Here we enter Piazza San Firenze.

PIAZZA SAN FIRENZE. — This is an attractive, typically Florentine piazza, where, at the far end, one side of the XV century Palazzo Vecchio can be seen, and at the other end is the fortress-like Palazzo del Bargello, whose XIII century tower contrasts with the slender campanile of the Badia, and the distant shape of the Brunelleschian cupola of the Cathedral. On the right again is the large PALAZZO GONDI, one of the best examples of the Florentine Renaissance, built by Giuliano da Sangallo in 1494, and has a very beautiful porticoed courtyard. Opposite is the complex Baroque edifice, from which the piazza takes its name. It consists of a palace with a church on each side. The Palace which has a XVII century facade, was once a Phillipine convent, and is now occupied by the Law Courts. The church on its left is dedicated to San Firenze.

NATIONAL MUSEUM OR BARGELLO

The Bargello Palace is thus named because toward the end of the 15th century the Captain of Justice (or Bargello) established himself here together with the city judges. The building, begun in 1256 (43 years before the Signoria Palace), was first the residente of the Captain of the People, then of the Mayor, and it is the most important civic building after the Signoria Palace. It has a typically mediaeval physiognomy with its tower called « La Volognana » proud and vigilant like a sentinel. The back part with the tower is the oldest and was built by the friars Sisto and Ristoro. The posterior section was built between 1260 and 1346 by the architects Neri di Fioravante and Benci di Cione, the same who constructed the courtyard and the splendid Council Room, worked on it. Inside the palace is the National Museum.

ARMS ROOM: Near the entrance to the palace. Various Medici arms from the 16th and 17th centuries. - COURTYARD: surrounded on three sides by a gallery, in which are various statues by artists of 15th century Florence. - Through a door in the courtyard one can enter the 13TH CENTURY ROOM, with the *Madonna and Child* by Tino di Camaino, and from there the MICHELANGELO ROOM which displays works by the great master: *Bacchus with small Satyr* (1497), *David* (1530), *bust of Brutus* (1540) and other important works. - Going up the master stairway we reach the porch with sculptures by Giambologna. - GENERAL COUNCIL ROOM: of extremely beautiful architecture, it contains works by Donatello, the great 14th century Florentine master: *Saint George, Crucifixion, David, Saint John the Baptist, Attis, bust of Giovanni Antonio da Narni, the Marzocco* and numerous other works. There are also other works by 14th century Florentine artists, all more or less influenced by Donatello: Desiderio da Settignano, Michelozzo, Brunelleschi, Ghiberti, Luca della Robbia and others. - MAJOLICA ROOM: examples from the old Italian workshops in Urbino, Pesaro, Faenza and Florence. - IVORIES ROOM: precious and rare objects which constitute one of the richest existing collections of ivories. - VESTIBULE: enamels, and oriental, Venetian, 16th century French crystal vases. - PODESTÀ CHAPEL: frescoes attributed to

NATIONAL MUSEUM. — The Courtyard.

Giotto. Behind glass are illuminated 14th century prayer-books. - CELLINI ROOM: masterpieces of the unrivalled Florentine engraver and sculptor, among which, *the bronze bust of Cosimo I, Perseus freeing Andromeda, the Greyhound,* and the preliminary study of the *David* under the Loggia of the Signoria. On the walls, *terracottas* by Giovanni della Robbia. - After the ROOM OF SMALL BRONZES we reach the DELLA ROBBIA ROOM containing terracottas by Luca, Andrea and Giovanni. - VERROCCHIO ROOM: (Andrea de' Cioni, 1435-88), containing works of this great Florentine master, in whose workshop Leo-

NATIONAL MUSEUM. — Wedding Chest (15th century). Detail.

nardo da Vinci was formed. There are also works by Antonio Rossellino, Mino da Fiesole, Benedetto da Maiano, Antonio del Pollaiolo and others. - FIREPLACE ROOM (Sala del Camino): thus named because of the fireplace coming from the Borgherini Palace and sculpted by Benedetto da Rovezzano in the 16th century.

NATIONAL MUSEUM. — B. Ammannati: « Leda with the Swan ».

Dante's House.

CHURCH OF THE BADIA

The church was founded by Countess Wilma, mother of the Marquis Ugo of Tuscany, in the 10th century; subsequently it underwent many alterations until the 17th century. Of the old building only the b e a u t i f u l Romanesque campanile remains; ending in Gothic style, it produces an effect of rare harmony. The portal is by Benedetto da Rovezzano (1495) and has over it a terracotta by Benedetto Buglione, a pupil of the Della Robbia family. The atrium is also by Benedetto da Rovezzano.

THE INTERIOR of the church is in the form of a Greek Cross, with a remarkably beautiful ceiling by Matteo Segaloni. There are some important works of the Tuscan Renaissance: to the right, the *Pandolfini tomb* by Bernardo Rossellino; the *Madonna with Child and Saints*, a bas-relief by Mino da Fiesole; the *tomb of Bernardo Giugni* by Mino da Fiesole. To the left, the *tomb of Count Ugo*, Marquis of Tuscany, by Mino da Fiesole. Inside the small chapel on the left, the frescoes are by a disciple of Giotto and attest that this is the oldest part of the building. Toward the exit is the masterpiece of Filippino Lippi, the *Madonna appearing to Saint Bernard* (1480). From the sacristy one can go to the CLOISTER OF

THE ORANGES with a series of 15th century frescoes of the *Life of Saint Bernard*.

On leaving the church and crossing Via del Proconsolo one can follow the Via Ghibellina, where at N. 70 is the house of the Buonarroti family.

CASA BUONARROTI. — This house was bought by Michelangelo, and his heirs transformed it into a museum in honour of their great ancestor. The museum is interesting because it contains the youthful works of Michelangelo, arranged in a room on the second floor: among which, the high relief of the *Battle of the Centaurs and the Lapithae*, of 1429, *the Madonna and Child*, also called the San Lorenzo Madonna, and others. In this room is also the original of a *portrait of Michelangelo*, a *bronze bust* by Daniele da Volterra. In the adjoining room is a collection of drawings: studies of nudes, compositions, portraits, not to mention architectural projections. In the other rooms: a *portrait of Michelangelo* by Bugiardini and the other one by Venusti; *a portrait of Vittoria Colonna*, the woman whom Michelangelo loved, attributed to Pontormo. On the first floor there are reproductions of works of Michelangelo not in Florence: *the Prisoners*, in the Louvre; *the Madonna*, in Bruges; *the Moses* in the Church of San Pietro in Vincoli in Rome; *the Rondanini Pietà*, in Milan and others.

Almost opposite the house, is Via delle Pinzochere, which soon leads into Piazza Santa Croce.

PIAZZA SANTA CROCE. — This piazza has followed the evolution of the Florentine traditions, from the first meetings of the people; when they listened to preachers expounding the teachings of Christ, to the 15th century jousts of the cavaliers, amongst which, that won by Giuliano de' Medici and immortalised by Poliziano, and to the 16th century games of football, in which the Florentine participated so enthusiastically. Of rectangular shape, the piazza has the facade of the church of Santa Croce as a backcloth, and is bounded by old palaces. Amongst these is, at No. 1 PALAZZO COCCHI SERRISTORI, constructed in 1470 by Baccio d'Agnolo, and at No. 21 PALAZZO DELL'ANTELLA, built in 1619 by Giulio Parigi. It has a polychrome facade and projecting upper storeys. The frescoes were painted in only 27 days by twelve artists, under the direction of Giovanni da San Giovanni.

CHURCH OF SANTA CROCE

A church of the Franciscan order, it remained until 1295 over the site of a small ancient church adjoining the Franciscan convent; it is attributed to Arnolfo di Cambio, the architect of the Signoria Palace and the cathedral. The facade is modern (1863) as is the campanile (1865), both maintaining the Gothic style. Since times of antiquity the Florentines, moved by the new and profound teachings of the Franciscan order, wished to be buried in this church so that, little by little, it became a great cemetery, and funeral monuments were erected, giving the church the character of a sacrarium of civic memories. It then became a national reliquary when, later, distinguished men in every field were buried here, and those not actually buried had funeral monuments to attest their spiritual presence.

Church of Santa Croce.

The INTERIOR is in the form of an Egyptian Cross divided into three naves by elegant pilasters and sharply pointed arches. The ceiling is opened to the roof with uncovered scaffolding while the walls were entirely decorated with frescoes by Giotto and his assistants, works which we could see today if Giotto Vasari, re-arranging the church on the orders of Cosimo I, had not had them plastered over, placing against them altars of very little worth. In the right nave is the *tomb of Michelangelo* by Vasari; *the cenotaph of Dante* by Ricci (1829); *the monument to Vittorio Alfieri* by Canova (1810). Near the first pilaster the rhythmic and delightful high relief by Antonio Rossellino, with the *Madonna of the Milk* (1478). Near the third pilaster is the remarkably beautiful pulpit by Benedetto da Maiano, with the *Scenes form the Life of Saint Francis* (1475). Near the wall, a *monument to Nicholas Machiavelli* by Innicenzo Spinazzi (1787). Further on an extremely

109

CHURCH OF SANTA CROCE. — Interior.

beautiful tabernacle in « pietra serena » with Donatello's masterpiece, the *Annunciation,* of 1430. The *tomb of the humanist historian Leonardo Bruni,* the work of Bernardo Rossellino (15th century); after it, the *tomb* of Gioacchino Rossini, the great musician. At this point the chapels begin. CHAPEL OF THE SACRAMENT: an important cycle of frescoes by Antonio Gaddi and pupils (14th century, the *Crucifix* by Niccolò Gerini (1383). GIUGNI CHAPEL: cycle of frescoes of the *Story of Mary* by Taddeo Gaddi (1332-38). Passing through a beautiful doorway by Michelozzo, we go to the 13th century SACRISTY with frescoes by Niccolò di Pietro Gerini (1380); inlaid wardrobes by Giovanni di Michele (1454) and Nanni Ungaro (1530), with precious illuminated himnals, sacred objects and reliquaries from the 14th and 15th centuries. Towards the back is the RINUCCINI CHAPEL with frescoes by Giovanni da Milano and pupils, of *Scenes form the Lives of Mary Magdalen and the Virgin Mary.* The panel on the altar is by Giovanni del Biondo (1379). In the corridor at the end, on the left is the NOVITIATE CHAPEL built by Michelozzo in 1434, with a beautiful marble tabernacle attributed to Donatello and a glazed terracotta by Andrea della Robbia. Returning to the church, the cycle of chapels continues, each one built by one of the major Florentine families. The first is the RICCARDI CHAPEL, with frescoes attributed to Cimabue;

110

CHURCH OF SANTA CROCE. — **Donatello:** « Annunciation ».

the second, also a RICCARDI CHAPEL with frescoes by
Giotto and a monument to Carlotta Bonaparte by Lorenzo
Bartolini. The fourth is the PERUZZI CHAPEL, frescoes by
Giotto and a *monument to Carlotta Bonaparte* by Lorenzo
executed circa 1317: particularly fine and famous is the
left fresco on the bottom of it *the death of Saint Francis.*
The Main, or ALBERTI CHAPEL is covered with frescoes of

111

SANTA CROCE. — Giotto: « Burial of St. Francis.

the *Legend of the Cross* by Agnolo Gaddi (1380). Next is the TOSINGHI CHAPEL, now called the Sloane Chapel, once frescoed by Giotto, of which remains only the *Annunciation;* on the altar, a polyptych by Giovanni del Biondo

SANTA CROCE. — Giotto: « Visions of Fra Augustine and Bishop Guido of Assisi ».

112

SANTA CROCE. — Giorgio Vasari: « Tomb of Michelangelo ».

MICHAELI ANGELO BONAROTIO
E VETUS SIMONIORUM FAMILIA
SCULPTORI PICTORI ET ARCHITECTO
OMNIBUS NOTISSIMO
LEONARDUS PATRUO AMANTISS ET DE SE OPTIME MERITO
TRANSLATIS ROMA EIUS OSSIBUS ATQUE IN HOC TEMPLO MAIOR
SUOR SEPULCRO CONDITIS COHORTANTE SERENIS COSMO MED
MAGNO HETRURIAE DUCE
P. C.
AN S MDLXV

The Pazzi Chapel.

(1372). Beside it, the CAPPNI CHAPEL dedicated to the *Italian Mother* with a *Pietà* by Libero Andreotti (1926). Following; the RICASOLI CHAPEL with frescoes and paintings by Luigi Sabatelli and his sons, of the 19th century; the BARDI CHAPEL with frescoes by Bernardo Daddi (14th century) and an altar-piece in polychrome terracotta by Giovanni della Robbia; the BARDI DI VERNI CHAPEL with frescoes by Maso di Banco, called Giottino; the NICCOLINI CHAPEL, the last in the transept, devoted to the *Assumption of the Virgin,* with frescoes by Volterrano (1660); the BARDI CHAPEL with Donatello's *Crucifix* (1425), criticized by Brunelleschi who thought it was too realistic; the SALVIATI CHAPEL with the beautiful *tomb of Princess Zamojska* by Lorenzo Bartolini (1937). At the end of the left nave is the *tomb of Carlo Marsuppini* by Desiderio da Settignano (15th century). Beyond, the *memorial stones* of Lorenzo and Vittorio Ghiberti and the *tomb of Galileo Galilei,* by G.B. Foggini (1437).

PAZZI CHAPEL

To the right of Santa Croce is a 13th century cloister with frescoes of *Stories of Saint Francis,* from the 14th century; at the end one can see that Renaissance jewel, the Pazzi Chapel, in all its incomparable harmony and balanced

Antonio Rossellino:
« The Madonna of the Milk ».

Giorgio Vasari:
« Tomb of Michelangelo ».

grace. Brunelleschi built it and worked from 1430 until 1446. The external arcade has a frieze with *heads of cherubims* by Desiderio da Settignano and the majolica decorations are by Luca della Robbia; the *Saint Andrew* over the majolica decorations of Giuliano da Maiano. The interior is exceptionally simple with the typical Brunelleschian decoration in pietra serena on white plaster. The only note of colour is in the medaillions by Luca della Robbia.

SANTA CROCE MUSEUM (Museo dell'Opera). — From the cloister one can reach the museum, which was the refectory of the convent and where are kept architectural fragments, remains of frescoes, and sculptures and paintings of various artists, all coming from the church. Especially beautiful is the Saint Ludovic of Toulouse (1423), a bronze statue by Donatello.

BARDINI MUSEUM. — This museum is interesting for its collection of works of exceptional importance. Donated to the city of Florence by the antiquarian, Stefano Bardini, it is a modern building nevertheless curious and interesting with its windows formed from originals on altars in a church in Pistoia. Among the artists represented we will cite Tino da Camaino, Antonio del Pollaiuolo, Michelozzo, Andrea della Robbia, Donatello, Benedetto da Rovezzano and others.

SEVENTH ITINERARY

Viale dei Colli - Piazzale Michelangelo - Church of San Miniato al Monte - Forte Belvedere (Fortress).

PIAZZALE MICHELANGELO

Having visited the museums, churches, and works of art in which Florence is so rich, it is indispensable, as in a stupendous recapituation which sums up all of the natural and artistic beauties of this city and its surroundings to see the magnificent Viale dei Colli which ends in the enormous and beautiful Piazzale Michelangelo, from which one can have an incomparable wiev of the panorama of Florence. Piazzale Michelangelo constitutes the most sug-

View of Florence from Piazzale Michelangelo.

Piazzale Michelangelo.

gestive and evocative point of the famous drive or walk along the Viale dei Colli. There one can enjoy a complete view of the city, cut in two by the Arno. In the middle of the square there is a monument dedicated to Michelangelo with a synthesis of the most celebrated works sculpted by that incomparable artist: the *David* in the middle, and, around the pedestal, the four statues which adorn the Medici tombs in the Chapels of the same name. Piazzale Michelangelo can be reached either from Porta Romana, or from Piazza Francesco Ferrucci after the San Niccolò bridge or from other streets which provide typical walks or drives with fragments of the Florentine panorama framed in the green of the trees and the tall and slender cypresses. This marvellous appendix to the beauties of Florence is the work of the architect Giuseppe Poggi, who conceived of and built it in 1863.

CHURCH OF SAN SALVATORE AL MONTE. — Near Piazzale Michelangelo, at the beginning of Viale Galileo, climbing the ramp among the cypresses, one can find the Church of San Salvatore, built by Cronaca (1475) and called by Michelangelo « la bella villanella », for that particular grace which it emanates. Renaissance in form, inside it has a Della Robbia terracotta of the *Deposition*, and painted altars of the 15th century.

CHURCH OF SAN MINIATO AL MONTE

A building which, together with the Baptistery, is one of the very rare examples of Florentine-Romanesque architecture. The building of the church began in the 11th century and it was finished in the 13th century; it is typical, with its facade covered with white and dark green marbles and the mosaic of the 12th century with *Christ between the Madonna and Saint Miniato,* which, when the sun shines on it, sends reflecting beams from its golden background.

THE INTERIOR is in three naves divided by columns. In the central nave the floor is carved with the signs of the zodiac, lions and doves.At the end of the central nave is the small *Crucifix Chapel,* the work of Michelozzo (1377) The painted panels inside the chapel are by Agnolo Gaddi From the right nave the presbytery can be reached by a flight of stairs, with its stupendous transennas and magnificent pulpit; the latter is a noteworthy example of Florentine-Romanesque. The sacristy has frescoes by Spinello Aretino of towards the end of the 14th century with *Scenes from the Life of Saint Benedict;* From here one can return to the presbytery in order to visit the semicircular apse with its columns and arches in black marble. The mosaic in the vault depicts *Christ giving his blessing.* Going down the stairway in the left nave, to the right is the CHAPEL OF THE CARDINAL OF PORTUGAL, built by

View from the Piazzale Michelangelo.

The Synagogue. Oriental style (1872-74).

Church of San Miniato.

Antonio Manetti (1459-66) for the Cardinal Archbishop of Lisbon, Jacopo di Lusitania. The medallions in the vault depict the *Cardinal Virtues and the Holy Spirit,* the works of Luca della Robbia. In the recess to the right the *tomb* of the Cardinal is the work of Antonio Rossellino; to the left, over the EPISCOPAL CHAIR, an *Annunciation* by Alessio Baldovinetti (1467). The panel on the altar is a copy of the original by Antonio and Piero del Pollaiolo, now kept in the Uffizi Gallery.

FORTE BELVEDERE

It was built by Giovanni de' Medici and B. Buontalenti in 1590-95. It is composed of a main building with two magnificent wings, from which there is a wonderful view of the town. The little palace of the fort houses an EXHIBITION OF DETACHED FRESCOES, which have come from various places and are particularly valuable. Amongst them are the *Deluge* and *Noah's Sacrifice* by Paolo Uccello; the *Annunciation* by Botticelli; a *St. Girolamo* by Piero della Francesca; the *Story of St. Benedict,* by the so-called Master of the Courtyard of Oranges; and also works by Taddeo Gàddi, Maso di Banco, Andrea Orcagna and others.

FIESOLE. — **View from the road leading to the Church of St. Francis.**

FIESOLE. — **Façade of the Church of St. Farncis.**

FIESOLE

From Florence to Fiesole the route is one of the most suggestive imaginable. It unwinds among a continuous succession of unforgettable views, across rows of cypresses and very beautiful villas. Beyond SAN DOMENICO, Florence appears at the bottom of the valley in all of its enchanting beauty.

THE CATHEDRAL

Dedicated to Saint Romolo, it was begun in 1028 and enlarged successively in 1256 and 1300. The interior is in three naves divided by columns coming from pagan temples. The SALUTATI CHAPEL is important, with the *tomb of the Bishop Salutati* near the right wall, the work of Mino da Fiesole. Also by the latter, near the left wall, is the altar reredos with *Madonna and Child*.

ROMAN THEATRE

The entrance is behind the apse of the cathedral. It is typically Greek. It was discovered in 1809 and excavated in 1873. It goes back to the time of Silla, but in the 1st and 3rd centuries A.D. it was enriched. Near the theatre the Baths are visible; they are also of the time of Silla. A small road going west leads to the Etrusco-Roman temple; to the right one can see the remains of an Etruscan door, together with remains of the walls, also Etruscan.

FIESOLE. — Roman Amphitheatre.

FIESOLE MUSEUM. — Contains for the most part objects found in excavation of the territory of, and around Fiesole. Etruscan tombs, fragments of architectural decorations. Etruscan and Latin inscriptions, bronzes, coins and objects from the barbaric and medieval periods. Of exceptional interest, in the second room, is a small statue of Ionic-Etruscan origins depicting *Hercules,* and the Etruscan mirror with the *Sacrifice of Polyxena.* In the third room is the head of a *statue of Claudius.*

BANDINI MUSEUM. — Contains very beautiful terracottas by the Della Robbia family, of the 15th and 16th centuries, and furnishing of the 14th and 15th centuries. Especially important are the works of Ambrogio Lorenzetti, Jacopo del Sellaio, Neri di Bicci, Nardo di Cione, etc.

SAINT FRANCIS. — Before leaving Fiesole it is advisable to go up to the terrace of the church of Saint Francis. It can be reached by the path ascending sharply to the church, standing at the top of the hill. From the terrace, named after the church one can enjoy a stupendous and awe-inspiring view of Florence and its surroundings. Before leaving, visit the convent, the church, the cloister and the museum.

CERTOSA

From Via Porta Romana through Galluzzo, we reach the Carthusian Monastery rising high up between cypresses and olive trees like an ancient castle dominating the valley below where the two rivers, the Greve and the Ema join.

It was founded in 1341 by the Florentine Nicolò Acciaioli, grand seneschal of the kingdom of Naples and Viceroy of Puglia.

After having entered the courtyard, we are in front of the beautiful façade of the church with statues in terracotta. Over a staircase, on top of which is the fresco by Jacopo da Empoli with *Jesus Preaching*, we pass into another courtyard and into a small chapel with the *Holy Family* by Andrea del Sarto, and from here we go into the church dedicated to Saint Lawrence. This church, in accordance with the Carthusian rite, in divided into two parts: one for the monks and one for the laymen. The choir seats were executed on the style of Angelo Feltrini (1591); the frescoes are by Poccetti, the sacred bronze vase on the high altar is by Giambologna.

In the chapels adjacent to the church are valuable paintings by Florentine artist of the 15th century among which is *Madonna and Saint* by Fra Angelico.

Going into the crypt, we find there the tombs of the family of the Acciaioli. Among them is the tomb of the founder of the monastery, Nicolò, which is believed to the work of Andrea Orcagna. The *sepulcral monument of the Cardinal Nicolò* is the work of Donatello and has been decorated by Giuliano da Sangallo. We now go into the *Purgatory of the Carthusian Monks* with interesting glass windows by Giovanni da Udine (1560) and through the small cloister we enter into the *Chapter Hall* with its beautiful fresco of the *Crucifixion* by Mariotto Albertinelli (1505). The tomb *slab of the Cardinal Buonafede*, with the figure of Death, is the work of Francesco da Sangallo (1545). The *Holy Virgin with Saints* is attributed to Andrea del Sarto.

In the *big Cloister* we find works by della Robbia, paintings by Pontormo and other artists of the 16th century.

We then reach the *Pharmacy of the Convent*, which has a high reputation for its famous liquors.

CHURCH OF ST. FRANCIS. — Cloister of St. Bernardin. ▶

CHURCH OF ST. FRANCIS. — Cosimo Rosselli: « Adoration
of the Magi ».

TIMETABLE OF MUSEUMS AND GALLERIES

STATE MUSEUM: opening hours

Summer: 9,30-16,30

Winter: 9,30-16   week days

	Entrance fee	Hours and fee holidays	Closed on
Galleria degli Uffizi Loggiato degli Uffizi, 6	L. 250	9,30-16 L. 125	Monday
Galleria Palatina Piazza Pitti, Palazzo Pitti	L. 200	9,30-16	Tuesday
Museo degli Argenti Piazza Pitti, Palazzo Pitti	—	9-13 L. 100	Tuesday
Appartamenti Monumentali Piazza Pitti, Palazzo Pitti	—	9-13	Tuesday
Galleria d'Arte Moderna Piazza Pitti, Palazzo Pitti	L. 150	9-13 L. 150	Tuesday
Galleria dell'Accademia Via Ricasoli, 52	L. 150	9-13 L. 75	Monday
Museo Nazionale (Bargello) Via del Proconsolo, 4	L. 150	9-13 L. 75	Tuesday
Museo di San Marco Piazza San Marco	L. 150	9-13 L. 75	Monday
Museo della Casa Fiorentina Antica - Piazza Davanzati, Palazzo Davanzati	L. 150	9-13 L. 75	—
Museo Archeologico Piazza SS. Annunziata, 9	L. 150	9-13 L. 100	—
Casa Buonarroti Via Ghibellina, 70	L. 100	9-13 L. 100	Tuesday
Opificio delle Pietre Dure Via degli Alfani, 78 Saturdays 9,30-12,30. Saturday and Sunday 9,30-16,30	L. 100	9,30-12,30 L. 50	
Cappelle Medicee (Tombe di Michelangelo) Piazza Madonna Summer: 9-17 Winter: 9-16	L. 160	9,30-12,30 L. 80	—
Giardino di Boboli Piazza Pitti Summer: 9-18,30 Winter: 9-16,30	—	Free	—
Museo della Fondazione Horne Via dei Benci, 6	Open on Mondays and Thursdays Entrance fee L. 100.		

Ring the bell for visiting the following:

	Entrance fee	Entrance fee holidays
Cenacolo di Andrea del Sarto a San Salvi - Via A. del Sarto, 16	L. 100 *	L. 50
Cenacolo di Santa Apollonia Via XXVII Aprile, 1	free	free